GET RID OF WORKS…

GROW

PARTS OF SPEECH

USER-FRIENDLY GAMES & ACTIVITIES FOR ELEMENTARY-LEVEL LANGUAGE INSTRUCTION

Debbie Hisam & Linda Seth

etc. publications

ACKNOWLEDGMENTS

The authors of GROW: Parts of Speech would very much like to thank the classroom teachers of Belmont Elementary School in Belmont, West Virginia and St. Marys Elementary School in St. Marys, West Virginia. These teachers have opened their classrooms to us for many years so that we might attempt to teach language skills in unconventional ways. These teachers have always been enthusiastic about our language lessons and without their support we would not have had the opportunity to implement our ideas for language instruction and intervention.

The authors would also like to thank all of the students of St. Marys Elementary and Belmont Elementary who so warmly welcomed us into their weekly routines. These students eagerly anticipated our lessons and greeted us with warm smiles and heartfelt cheers. Responses and feedback from these children provided us with insight into the strengths and weaknesses of our lessons so that we could modify activities to obtain maximum results.

A special thank you goes to Mary Jane Helgren who modified and finalized our cover design.

Our sincere appreciation goes to Kristi Venderlic and Martha Hockenberry for their many hours of proofreading. Their assistance was invaluable.

An enormous thank you is extended to our families. They have given us the time and space that we needed to complete this wonderful, yet time consuming project.

L. S. and D. H.

Printed in the U.S.A.

For more information from etc. publications:
RR 1 Box 24 A, Friendly, West Virginia 26146
e-mail: GROWetc@hotmail.com

Books in this series:
GROW: Parts of Speech (1998)
Vocabulary GROWth (2000)

Printed by Easton Printing Company
Parkersburg, WV

INTRODUCTION

GROW: Parts of Speech is a collection of activities designed for classroom teachers and specialists to teach and/or reinforce language skills as they relate to parts of speech. These activities have been developed by two public school speech therapists with a combined total of 43 years of experience in the public school system. The authors have been providing whole class language lessons in the regular classroom for a total of 22 years, and they are anxious to share their successes. With today's educational emphasis on collaborative teaching and cooperative learning, the activities in this book are invaluable. This book is truly unique.

The lessons included in GROW are fun and interesting for both teachers and students, and they are definitely a break from the norm. Exercises have been designed to be easily used by classroom teachers and speech therapists who provide large or small group language intervention. Collaborative teaching becomes easy!

All necessary materials, except regular classroom supplies, such as pencils and paper, are included in GROW. Only a few pages will require duplication before using.

Lessons are designed for 30 minute sessions, but enough materials are given to extend. Because there is usually a surplus of sentences, phrases or words on provided lists, teachers may select those that will best meet their needs, rather than following in any particular order.

The target population for GROW lessons is generally first through fifth graders. Some resource classes could also benefit. Each activity is designed to involve every student.

When grouping children for GROW activities, do so according to ability levels. This will result in better cooperative learning and more equitable chances of performance.

Most GROW activities can be easily adapted to a variety of game or non-game formats. Alternative methods for performing each activity are suggested under MODIFICATIONS by narration or by symbols. Complete explanations of these symbols can be found in the ACTIVITY MODIFICATION SYMBOLS section of this book. Choose your favorite!

Many activities are also easily adapted to other parts of speech, as suggested in the Table of Contents, but word lists and other necessary resources will not have been provided.

GROW lessons address many skills unrelated to parts of speech, such as vocabulary development, following directions, cooperative teamwork, and independent decision making. OBJECTIVES for each activity can be individually reviewed for more specific information.

The authors of this book feel strongly that there are many fun, nontraditional ways to be successful in the classroom without being tied to workbooks. This is the reason for the publication of GROW: Parts of Speech. Enjoy!

TABLE OF CONTENTS

✓ Primary Targets

● Could Be Adapted For (no lists provided)

✓ Primary Targets

● Could Be Adapted For (no lists provided)

	PAGE #	NOUNS	VERBS	PRONOUNS	ADJECTIVES	ADVERBS	PREPOSITIONS	CONJUNCTIONS	INTERJECTIONS	REVIEW
PRONOUNS										
NOUN, PRONOUN, NEITHER	31	✓		✓						
NOUN/PRONOUN SUBSTITUTION	33	✓		✓						
PRONOUN DETECTIVE	35	●	●	✓	●	●	●	●		
I SPY A PRONOUN	37	●		✓	●	●	●	●	●	
ADJECTIVES										
GO TOGETHERS	39	✓	●		✓	●				
HEADLINE NEWS	41				✓					
ONE DESCRIBES BOTH	42	✓			✓	●				
ADJECTIVE DETECTIVE	43	●	●	●	✓	●	●	●		
IT'S ALL THE SAME	45		●		✓					
DESCRIBE IT TO THE LETTER	47				✓					
ADJECTIVE CHALLENGE	48	✓			✓					
PICTURE THIS	49	✓			✓					
COMPARE THESE	50				✓					
A-B-C ADJECTIVE	51	●	●		✓	●				
ADVERBS										
I SPY AN ADVERB	52	●		●	●	✓	●	●	●	
CAN YOU VERB ADVERBLY?	53		✓			✓				
ADVERB BINGO	55			●	●	✓	●	●	●	
ADJECTIVE, ADVERB, NEITHER	57				✓	✓				
ADVERB CHARADES	59		●		●	✓				
HOW'D THEY DO THAT?	60					✓				
MOVABLE ADVERBS	61					✓				

√ Primary Targets

● Could Be Adapted For (no lists provided)

ACTIVITY MODIFICATION SYMBOLS

🗁 WORD BANK: When the class generates a list of words of a particular type, such as adjectives, synonyms..., write the list on chart paper, label it, and hang it in the classroom. Encourage students to utilize this vocabulary list for creative writing assignments.

❄ COOPERATIVE TEAMWORK: Students are divided into teams and given a task. After a team conference one student from each group records its answer and waits his turn to present the team's response to the class. Team points may be awarded for correct responses.

⌘ TIC TAC TOE: On the chalkboard draw a standard 3 x 3 tic tac toe grid, or for more of a challenge, a 4 x 4 grid. Label each square with clues designed to elicit the targeted words, or with numbers which refer to a list of clues for targeted words. Divide the class into two teams and alternate turns between them. If a student gives a correct response, he places his team's symbol (X or O) in the appropriate square on the grid. The first team to earn three squares in a row wins the game. (See NOUN TIC TAC TOE for further instructions.)

SENTENCE TIC TAC TOE: On the chalkboard draw a 4 x 4 (or 5 x 5) grid. Use this format for targeting two particular types of words, such as nouns and verbs, or adverbs and verbs. Along the top of the grid print 4 (or 5) words that fit one of the categories. Down the left side of the grid print 4 (or 5) words that fit the second category being targeted. To earn a particular space for his team a player must use the word written above his space and the word written to the left of his space in a single meaningful, grammatically correct sentence. (See SENTENCE TIC TAC TOE-NOUN/VERB for further instructions.)

☺☹ SMILEY FACE/SAD FACE CARDS: Give each student one smiley face and one sad face card. Instruct students that the smiley face card indicates a "yes" answer, and the sad face card means "no". Tell each student to select the answer card which indicates his response, and to hold that card close to his chest. No responses should be visible until the entire class is instructed to simultaneously raise the cards. At a glance it is then easy to see which students are having difficulty with the targeted concepts.

⚐ FOOTBALL: Divide the class into two teams. On the chalkboard draw a football field with ten 10-yard line markings. Put one team's name on each end of the field. Use a magnet or self-stick note to represent the football, and place it in the middle of the field.

Alternate teams when eliciting responses. For each correct response move the "ball" 10 yards closer to the answering team's goal. For each incorrect response, subtract 10 yards. When a team reaches the zero yard line, tally six points and return the "ball" to the 50 yard line. Begin again with the nonscoring team.

BASEBALL: On the chalkboard draw a diamond-shaped playing field. Label the corners as "home", "1", "2", and "3". Choose different magnets or restickable notes to represent each of the teams. Move these markers around the "playing field" as players from each team give correct responses. Each time a team's marker lands on or passes "home", a run (one point) is scored. (See BATTER UP for further instructions.)

Questions may have up to three parts, such as "Name a common, plural noun". If correct, award three bases. If partially correct, award one base per correct component.

An alternate way to play this game would be to weight the questions by difficulty level, stating ahead of time how many bases can be earned by a particular question.

RAISE YOUR CARDS: This is a response mode which can be utilized to quickly and easily view all students' responses. This format can be used only when the same 2-4 choices of responses are required each time.

Give each student each of the needed number cards. On the chalkboard designate the response that each number represents. For example, #1 means "noun", #2 means "verb", and #3 means "adjective". When each student has selected one card to indicate his response, say "Raise your cards", and all students simultaneously do so. It is then easy to identify students who understand the goal and those who do not. If desired, team points may be earned by individuals who respond correctly.

BEE: This format is that of a traditional spelling bee. Place two teams in lines facing each other, and alternate questions between them. Only the person whose turn it is may respond. If correct, he remains standing. If incorrect, he must sit down. The team with the last player (or the most players) left standing at the end of play is the winner.

CIRCULAR BEE: Arrange students in a circle around the room. Announce that anyone who is wearing blue jeans (or brown shoes, glasses, jewelry...) must sit down in his place on the circle. Ask a question and choose any standing student to respond. Continue searching for correct responses by choosing standing students in order around the circle. If a student's response is incorrect, he must sit down in his place. After all standing students have had a correct response, announce that all standing students must sit and all sitting students must stand. Choose a student to answer the first question and proceed as in the first round.

Playing in this fashion gives students who are having difficulty with a particular concept twice the number of chances to respond.

WRITING INDEPENDENTLY: Each student records his own response on paper. Team points may be awarded for correct responses, if desired.

TICKETS: Divide the class into teams for a task. Choose one person from each team to be the respondent for the first question. Bring all respondents to the front of the class and give each three tickets (pieces of construction paper...). Remove one ticket from each respondent with each guess. When a student is out of tickets he may no longer make a guess. When the correct response is finally given, begin a new question with each new respondent beginning with three tickets. Team points may be awarded if desired.

ANSWERING ALOUD: This response mode may be used whether or not team points are being awarded. Responses may or may not be written before being presented aloud.

DETECTIVES: When working cooperatively as teams on an activity, each t*eam* is allowed to record only one answer. Points are awarded for correct responses, *but only if no other team selects the same response.*

When working *individually* to score points for teams, each *student* is allowed to record one answer. Each student will earn one point for his team if his response is correct, *and three or fewer classmates have chosen the same answer.* In this way as many as three points could be awarded to a particular team for any one question, or three teams may earn one point each... If four or more students in the class record the same answer, no points are scored for any team. When using this format be certain that teams have equal numbers of players for equal scoring opportunities. If teams are uneven, designate one person from each of the "shorted" teams as a "double respondent". This person is permitted to give two answers to each question. (See ADJECTIVE DETECTIVE for additional details.)

LET

THE

GAMES

BEGIN!

NAME THAT NOUN

OBJECTIVES:
To increase usage and understanding of nouns.
To increase usage and understanding of adjectives.
To improve auditory memory.
To improve vocabulary skills.
To improve analytical thinking.

TARGET POPULATION: Grades 2-5

MATERIALS: Noun/adjective list (provided)

PROCEDURE: Divide the class into two teams. The object of this game is for players to guess the secret noun from the clues provided. Clue #1 always tells whether the secret word is a person, place or thing. The other four clues are adjectives that describe the secret word.

The first player on Team #1 tells which numbered clue (1-5) she wants to hear. Read only that clue and give her 15 seconds to make a guess based on that clue alone. If she guesses correctly, her team is awarded 5 points. If her guess is incorrect, the first player on Team #2 chooses another clue to be revealed. Remind students to consider the previous clue(s), as well as the new one. That player also has 15 seconds to make her guess. If she is correct, the team is awarded 4 points. If the guess is incorrect, play passes to the second player on Team #1. The third clue is chosen and the clue is read. Three points are awarded for a correct guess. The fourth clue, if needed, would earn 2 points, and if the secret noun is not guessed until after the fifth clue, only 1 point is earned. If no one guesses the word, review all the clues and then tell the answer. Award no points in that case.

When a correct guess is made, record the appropriate number of points and choose a new secret noun. Begin round two with the next player on Team #2. Play continues until each student has had one or more turns.

MODIFICATIONS: Allow team members to review aloud the previously given clues, if help is needed by the guessing player, or write revealed clues on the board to help everyone.

The game could be played by having one person from each team come to the front of the class. Alternate giving clues to these two players until the correct answer is guessed or until all five clues have been given. If players do not guess correctly after all five clues have been revealed, allow each to call upon one player from her respective team to take a last guess.

NAME THAT NOUN
Noun/Adjective List

TIGER
1. thing
2. sleek
3. striped
4. ferocious
5. feline

MOUNTAIN
1. place
2. high
3. rugged
4. snowcapped
5. wooded

PRESIDENT
1. person
2. powerful
3. elected
4. respected
5. American

HAMMER
1. thing
2. useful
3. strong
4. hard
5. clawed

ROSE
1. thing
2. pretty
3. red
4. thorny
5. fragrant

COCOA
1. thing
2. liquid
3. chocolatey
4. delicious
5. hot

DINOSAUR
1. thing
2. huge
3. powerful
4. extinct
5. reptilian

KANGAROO
1. thing
2. flatfooted
3. jumpy
4. marsupial
5. Australian

MOON
1. place
2. distant
3. glowing
4. round
5. heavenly

PINE TREE
1. thing
2. bushy
3. prickly
4. woody
5. evergreen

DESERT
1. place
2. barren
3. dry
4. sandy
5. hot

REFRIGERATOR
1. thing
2. useful
3. boxy
4. large
5. cold

BICYCLE
1. thing
2. foot-powered
3. practical
4. fun
5. two-wheeled

POLICE
1. person
2. official
3. helpful
4. brave
5. uniformed

HELICOPTER
1. thing
2. airborn
3. wingless
4. exciting
5. military

CITY
1. place
2. crowded
3. busy
4. noisy
5. large

GRAPEFRUIT
1. thing
2. yellow
3. tangy
4. citrus
5. juicy

MOVIE STAR
1. person
2. talented
3. glamorous
4. famous
5. wealthy

FIREWORKS
1. thing
2. explosive
3. dangerous
4. loud
5. colorful

HOSPITAL
1. place
2. clean
3. medical
4. helpful
5. caregiving

CLOUD
1. thing
2. puffy
3. white
4. fluffy
5. high

SNAKE
1. thing
2. legless
3. scaley
4. cold blooded
5. slithery

RAINFOREST
1. place
2. tropical
3. green
4. humid
5. lush

COMPUTER
1. thing
2. high-tech
3. expensive
4. mechanical
5. multimedia

HEART
1. thing
2. internal
3. pumping
4. muscular
5. continuous

NOUN DETECTIVE

OBJECTIVES: To improve usage and understanding of nouns.
To improve vocabulary skills.
To improve strategies for success.
To improve auditory memory skills.
To improve listening skills.
To improve independent decision making.
To improve analytical thinking.

TARGET POPULATION: Grades 2-5

MATERIALS: Sentence list (provided)
Paper and pencil for each student

PROCEDURE: Divide students into teams. Provide each student with a piece of paper and a pencil. Explain that students will be writing down one, *and only one*, noun from the sentence that will be read. If teams cannot be divided evenly, it will be necessary to declare someone from each of the "shorted" teams to be the "double respondent". This person can write two nouns for each sentence, or teammates can take turns being the "double respondent". This ensures that all teams are given an equal number of responses per sentence. Students will be working independently but scoring points for their teams.

Read a sentence from the provided list three times so that no one must ask for repetition. Explain that team points will be kept, and that points will be earned as follows: If a student writes a word that is actually used as a noun in the given sentence, *and no more than three students from the class* have chosen that same noun, each of the students who has written that noun scores one point for his team. It is possible that all of the points may go to the same team. Explain to students that it is to their advantage to choose a noun that they think few others will choose. Copying a noun that someone else has written will decrease the chances of scoring points.

After reading the sentence three times, and all students are ready with one written noun, begin checking responses. Reread the sentence with a pause between each word. When the student hears the teacher say the word that he has written, he must immediately raise his hand or be left out of the count. Tally each point as it is earned. Be sure to inform students which words are nouns in the sentence even if no one has selected a particular noun. Also explain why incorrect responses are not nouns in that sentence.

Continue by reading the next sentence three times and following the same procedure. The team with the most points at the end of the session is declared the winner.

MODIFICATIONS: Deduct a point from a team if one of its members writes a word that is not used as a noun in the given sentence.

NOUN DETECTIVE

Sentence List

My Christmas tree came from a store in Florida that sells only special items.

Susan ran three miles to get help for the victims of the car wreck.

Flowers were planted by the kids in second grade who brought in packages of seeds.

On the top of my dresser is a gold watch that my dad won at the state fair.

If drivers would be more careful, people would not have so many accidents on the road.

Mom bought me a notebook, some pencils, some crayons and a ruler for school.

In the middle of the winter we like to build snowmen and to ride on sleds.

The TV announcer said that rain, snow and ice are in the forecast for Tuesday.

My big black dog lost his red collar in the mud last Friday after school.

On our way to the manager's office my dad hit a small deer that ran in front of our car.

Why did your teacher give homework to the class on a special day like Halloween?

My family went to the beach with Jim and his wife on our last vacation.

The vet told Dad that our sick dog should stay in the house, drink fluids, and take his medication.

The horse that won the race was given a gold medal and a wreath of flowers to put around his neck.

My new robe has a few stripes and some dots, but its pockets are a solid color.

Betsy left a light turned on in the kitchen window so the kids could see the path to the barn.

Mark built a deck on the front of his new house in the city of Belmont.

When Gary got his new car he filled it with gas and oil and went for a ride in the country.

Grandma picked out a couch and a chair that would look good in her living room or den.

Sam got in the refrigerator to get some apple juice, a ham sandwich and some cherry jello.

My sister swept the carpet, washed the dishes and made the beds on the second floor.

On Sunday the Smith family will go to the mountains, the park or the beach.

David put his comb and brush on his dresser and then he went to Mom's room to get her mirror.

Amy sits in the corner of the room in math class, beside her best friend.

The school bus driver closed his doors, turned on his lights, beeped his horn, and started down the road.

THE PROPER PATROL

OBJECTIVES: To improve usage and understanding of nouns.
To improve vocabulary skills.
To improve teamwork and cooperation.
To improve listening skills.
To improve strategies for success.

TARGET POPULATION: Grades 3-5

MATERIALS: Sentence list (provided)
Badges-copy from appendix
Tape

PROCEDURE: Read the following script to the class: "The Proper Patrol is an elite group of police officers which is not at all interested in lowly everyday common persons, places or things. Their job is to make certain that all of the proper persons, places and things get their proper respect. They must imprison anyone who treats these proper persons, places and things improperly. They must also arrest persons who try to elevate those lowly common persons, places and things to a proper position. Be prepared to be arrested by the Proper Patrol if you break one of its rules."

Divide the class into three or four teams and seat them in rows. Begin by choosing one person from each team to act as a patrolman. Give each patrolman a badge and send them to an area where they can easily confer. Designate a "prison" area, or tell students that if they are "arrested" they are to sit on the floor near their seats.

Begin with team #1. Tell them a noun from the provided list and then read the sentence which includes that noun. Without advice from teammates, the first player from team #1 must state if the given noun in the sentence was common or proper. The Proper Patrol then confers and announces its decision about the correctness of the response. If there is disagreement within the Patrol, the ultimate decision is made by the patrolman who was originally a part of the responding team. The Proper Patrol will annnounce if the given response was correct, in which case the respondent remains "free", or incorrect, in which case the respondent is sent to "prison".

The same procedure is continued with player #1 from team #2, player #1 from team #3... until the activity is concluded.

Function as prison warden in keeping control of the Proper Patrol. If a Proper Patrolman makes an incorrect decision and incorrectly sends or fails to send an individual to prison, thus showing that he does not know the proper laws, he is relieved of his duties and imprisoned himself. Replace him with a "free" teammate. When any one team is totally imprisoned, except for the Proper Patrolman, round one of the game is over. The warden counts the number of prisoners from each team and records the numbers on the chalkboard. These numbers represents the number of years that each team must spend in prison. More years can be added if additional rounds of the game are played.

If time allows, start round two by releasing all prisoners and choosing new patrolmen. Begin with the player who would have been next in round one.

When the final round has been played, calculate the total number of years that each team must serve. The winner is the team that receives the lightest sentence (i.e., the least number of points).

MODIFICATIONS: To keep Proper patrolmen from giving intentionally bad advice to the patrolman who is ultimately responsible for the decision, the warden may decide to sentence <u>each</u> team to an extra year when any patrolman makes an incorrect decision.

❄ ✋ ⚐ 🗐 ♈ ⌘ ☺☹

THE PROPER PATROL
Noun/Sentence List

HOUSE	We painted our house last summer.	(C)
ROSE	Mom, Dad and Rose went out to dinner.	(P)
COWBOYS	I hope the Cowboys win today's game.	(P)
NEWSPAPER	Please cut that coupon out of the newspaper.	(C)
ROSEMARY	The chef added salt, rosemary and garlic to the recipe.	(C)
MOOSE	Mom read us a story about a moose.	(C)
THANKSGIVING	Thanksgiving is a time for families to be together.	(P)
FLORIDA	It took about twelve hours to get to Florida.	(P)
MATH	I've always done very well in math.	(C)
SPRING	Every spring we plant a garden.	(C)
CAT	My pet's name is Top Cat.	(P)
CHILDREN	Mom wants me to play with those children.	(C)
JUNE	Her father's birthday is June 1st.	(P)
BILL	Our electric bill came today.	(C)
FRIDAY	I generally go skating on Friday nights.	(P)
HOSPITAL	My mother is a patient at Marietta Memorial Hospital.	(P)
FLOWERS	I went to the ballet with Susan Flowers.	(P)
ANGELS	Some people do not believe in angels.	(C)
CHICAGO	We drove through Chicago on our trip west.	(P)
MAPLE	The Smiths used to live on Maple Avenue.	(P)
MARCH	We went into town to join the march.	(C)
PRESIDENT	President Clinton visited with his daughter last month.	(P)
COMPUTER	Turn the computer off when you are finished.	(C)
BOWL	The Super Bowl will be played in January.	(P)
HOME	I love to watch the TV show *Home Improvement*.	(P)
CEMETERY	Tom and Lisa live to the north of the old cemetery.	(C)
CHEERIOS	Don't forget to buy some more Cheerios today.	(P)
ANDREW	Please pick up Andrew at seven o'clock.	(P)
MOTHER	Nathan gave his mother a big kiss.	(C)
RADIO	I listen to my favorite music on the radio.	(C)
PIZZA	Do you want to meet me at Pizza Hut?	(P)
AIRPORT	At the Pittsburgh Airport parking is difficult.	(P)
SUMMER	They named the baby Summer Michelle.	(P)
SCHOOL	I attend Belmont Elementary School.	(P)
MARK	Who put this black mark on my book?	(C)
DAD	I hope Dad remembers to pick up the mail.	(P)
MARS	Do you think that there is life on Mars?	(P)
DOG	They have a dog named Bo.	(C)
BUNNY	She hurried to see what the Easter Bunny left for her.	(P)
DOLLAR	We bought these new socks at Family Dollar.	(P)
WIZARD	An ugly wizard made the duck disappear.	(C)
SPOT	He saw Spot scratch me on the nose.	(P)
GIRL	Mom said I could join Girl Scouts.	(P)
MOVIE	Both boys went to the movie theater.	(C)

(C=common noun P=proper noun)

NOUN I.D.

OBJECTIVES:
- To improve usage and understanding of nouns.
- To improve auditory memory skills.
- To improve teamwork and cooperation.
- To improve vocabulary skills.
- To improve strategies for success.
- To improve listening skills.
- To improve analytical thinking.

TARGET POPULATION: Grades 2-5

MATERIALS: Sentence list (provided)
Paper and pencil for each team

PROCEDURE: Divide students into several teams and designate one person from each team as recorder. Each recorder must write down the general consensus of the group. Decide if the recorder will change after each task, periodically or not at all.

Read a sentence from the provided sentence list two or three times. Each group must record all words that it determines to be nouns in that sentence. When all groups are ready, or a given amount of time has elapsed, look at each group's list for scoring purposes. Quietly inform each team of the score it has earned, but at this point do not inform them how it was earned. When all team scores have been recorded, review the sentence with the class so that everyone can verify which words are indeed nouns.

Scoring is determined as follows: Each word on a team's list that was actually used as a noun in the sentence earns one point. One point is deducted for each word on the list that was not used as a noun in the sentence. No points are deducted for failing to include on the list some of the nouns from the sentence. For example, if the sentence actually had four nouns, and a team's list contains three words, two of which are correct nouns, the team earns one point. (Two correct minus one incorrect.) No team can score less than zero on any sentence. The team with the highest point total at the end of play is the winner.

MODIFICATIONS: 

NOUN I.D.
Sentence List

For Christmas Sally wants a bike and a doll.
My wonderful family lives in a dark green house.
When the snow falls, my dog tries to catch it in his mouth.
On Saturday the girls' grandmother will come to visit.
My birthday present was a bag of toys.
On Thursday morning our class will go on an exciting trip.
My son's teacher gave each child an apple.
Santa needs more help to finish his work.
I have a brand new bouncing baby brother.
Where did Jim put the bread and butter?
Dad went to the church program to tape my cousin.
When the telephone rang, Bill was in the shower.
On top of the stove is a grocery list for Mom.
The cat's collar fell off in the mud.
Where are you going?
The peaches on the tree still are not very ripe.
Honesty is important in this job.
On the left side of my dresser is a gold ring.
If it rains, the construction workers get a vacation.
A very ugly hairy ape ran across the slippery road.
A package under the front porch was already opened.
After Mom put the baby in the stroller, we went to the zoo.
My brown coat and blue gloves are on top of my locker.
Every Thanksgiving we have a great turkey dinner.
Some people finish their Christmas shopping early in December.
Missy walked to the graveyard to visit her uncle's grave.
After the clown did a flip, he stood on his head while he rode a horse.
Our school is collecting money to pay for our brand new playground.
The firemen rushed to the house, pulled out their hoses, and finally put the fire out.
When my homework is finished Mom said that I can play a game or watch TV.

NOUN SENSE OR NONSENSE

OBJECTIVES: To improve usage and understanding of nouns.
To improve vocabulary skills.
To improve strategies for success.
To improve teamwork and cooperation.

TARGET POPULATION: Grades 1-5

MATERIALS: Sentence list (provided)
Paper and pencil for each team

PROCEDURE: Divide students into teams, and designate one member of each team to be recorder. Choose a sentence from the provided list and notice if it is missing a person, a place or a thing. Without reading the sentence aloud, tell the class what is missing and instruct them to think of a noun that would fit that category. For example, if the sentence is, "Maria is holding a (thing) in her arms", tell each group to write down one "thing". Players should not use proper nouns since they will probably not fit well into the provided sentences.

When each team has written one noun that fits the category, read the sentence aloud to the class. Each team's recorder will then repeat the sentence and include its chosen noun. The team scores a point if its noun is in the designated category, and the class determines that the team's sentence makes sense.

When all nouns have been scored, continue with the next sentence. "Used" nouns may not be reused during the game. The team with the most points at the end of play wins.

MODIFICATIONS: For older students make the activity a little more challenging by having three blanks in each sentence. Each team must write one person, one place and one thing for each sentence, and hope that it makes sense.

Sentence List

Maria is holding a (thing) in her arms.
Her family visited a (place) in Ohio.
My (person) called me at home today.
Does anyone want to go to the (place)?
Joan went for a walk with her (person).
We saw a (thing) floating on the water.
Gary bought a present for his (person).
They went to the (place) to get a gift.
This (thing) will not fit in my car.
Danielle went inside the (place).
His (person) celebrated her 50th birthday.
Monica bought a (thing) at K-Mart.
A realtor is trying to sell that (place).
Did your (person) tell you that I called?
You look good in that (thing).
Sharon's (person) is only fifteen years old.
We were at the (place) when Dad found us.
Chris is not even as tall as a (thing).
Brandon ate a (thing) for lunch.
Your (person) likes to go swimming.

Modification Sentence List

I saw a (person) carrying a (thing) to the (place).
On the way to the (place) he drove past the (thing) that his (person) owns.
Did you tell the (person) to bring a (thing) to the (place)?
A (person) stopped by the (place) to pick up a (thing).
Your (thing) was not moved from the (place) by the (person).
At the (place) the (person) was eating a (thing).
Every Saturday my (person) brings a (thing) to the (place).

NOUN TICKETS

OBJECTIVES:
To improve usage and understanding of adjectives.
To improve usage and understanding of nouns.
To improve listening skills.
To improve vocabulary skills.
To improve strategies for success.
To improve analytical thinking.

TARGET POPULATION: Grades 2-5

MATERIALS: Noun list (provided)
3 Tickets per team-copy from appendix

PROCEDURE: Divide students into three teams. One person from each team is selected to be the ticket holder for the first round of play. Each ticket holder is given three tickets and sent out of hearing distance, such as in the hallway.

Select a noun from the provided list and reveal it to the remaining students. Then instruct the ticket holders to return to the classroom.

Ask non-ticket holders to raise their hands when they can think of an adjective that could be used to describe the secret noun. Select any student who is ready to respond, and ask him to state his describing word. Responses must be one-word adjectives only.

After hearing the first describing word, the first ticket holder, if any, to raise his hand has the opportunity to guess the secret noun. His guess will cost him one of his noun tickets. When a ticket holder spends all three of his tickets, he may no longer take a guess. If the ticket holder guesses the noun correctly, he scores one point for his team. If he was incorrect, another ticket holder may spend a ticket and take a guess. When no ticket holder wishes to continue guessing from that particular clue, select another student to provide an additional adjective that could be used to describe the secret noun. Remind students to think of both adjectives already given when trying to come up with the correct noun. Again the first ticket holder to raise his hand may spend a ticket and guess. Play on this noun continues until a ticket holder is correct, all tickets have been spent, or it is decided that too much time has been spent on that particular noun. If any non-ticket holder who is selected to provide an adjective actually states something other than an adjective, or uses more than one word, his ticket-holding teammate is not permitted to guess from that clue.

Begin round two by choosing new ticket holders from each group, sending them out of the room and revealing a new noun to those remaining. Continue until each student has been a ticket holder at least once. The team with the most points at the end of play is the winner.

MODIFICATIONS:   

Noun List

mask	saw	hair	sun	sidewalk	roller coaster
pizza	trash	fire	gun	elephant	refrigerator
dinosaur	water	fan	balloon	Santa	elevator
winter	snow	wheelchair	sky	computer	hamburger
puppy	doctor	ball	baby	pillow	cheese
mud	cave	popsicle	night	school	jail
celery	shirt	storm	skunk	music	medicine

TIC TAC NOUNS

OBJECTIVES:
- To improve usage and understanding of common nouns.
- To improve usage and understanding of proper nouns.
- To improve strategies for success.
- To improve teamwork and cooperation.

TARGET POPULATION: Grades 2-4

MATERIALS: Noun/Sentence list (provided)
Chalkboard and chalk

PROCEDURE: Draw on the chalkboard a Tic Tac Toe board. In each block write a different noun from the provided list. Write all words in capital letters. Divide the class into two teams, Team "X" and Team "O".

The first player from Team "X" chooses a noun from the board. Select one of the two provided sentences from the list and read it aloud. The player must then identify the given noun as either common or proper. If she is correct, she places her team's mark in the space where the chosen noun was located. If she is incorrect, no mark is made and play passes to the other team. The same procedure is continued with a player from Team "O". Play passes back and forth until one team has recorded three marks (X or O) in a row.

MODIFICATIONS: Instead of the conventional Tic Tac Toe grid, a 4 x 4 grid may be used that would require either four marks in a row, or a mark in each of the four corners to win.

TIC TAC NOUNS
Noun/Sentence List

FARMER	I got a ride to town from Mr. Farmer.	(P)
	The farmer grew corn and soybeans in his fields.	(C)
STORE	Mom bought my shoes at Murphy's Department Store.	(P)
	Will you go to the store for me?	(C)
AUNT	My aunt was in the hospital last week.	(C)
	I spent the night at Aunt Darla's house.	(P)
RANCH	The Johnson J-Bar Ranch is really huge.	(P)
	Sam worked at a dude ranch last summer.	(C)
MARCH	Dan went to Europe last year in March.	(P)
	The school band played a rousing march.	(C)
SUN	The sun was hidden by clouds all day.	(C)
	Ray bought a TV at Sun City Appliances.	(P)
FIELDS	The fields are full of deer each evening.	(C)
	He really likes Mrs. Fields' chocolate cake.	(P)
JACK	Our friend Jack is a helicopter pilot.	(P)
	I needed a jack to raise my car.	(C)
COFFEE	Sara spilled coffee on the rug.	(C)
	The new principal's name is Edward Coffee.	(P)
ISLAND	We went camping on the island.	(C)
	Manhattan Island is a very crowded place.	(P)
FLAG	The Steel City Flag Corps performed at the game.	(P)
	We say the pledge to the flag each day.	(C)
CEMETERY	The horses love the grass in the old cemetery.	(C)
	The Spruce Creek Cemetery is a spooky old place.	(P)
PIRATE	Pirate Pete had a wooden leg.	(P)
	The pirate had a pet parrot named Peggy Sue.	(C)
COWBOYS	The Dallas Cowboys lost the game this evening.	(P)
	The horse just kicked those cowboys!	(C)
MOON	The Blue Moon Cafe is open at noontime.	(P)
	The full moon was shining brightly.	(C)
CROSS	There's a beautiful cross on the church steeple.	(C)
	Holy Cross College is in the Midwest.	(P)
STREET	The race will end on Mulberry Street.	(P)
	You should park across the street.	(C)
KING	The enormous ruby belongs to the king.	(C)
	England's next monarch will be King Charles.	(P)
MUSTANG	Dad just bought a new Mustang convertible.	(P)
	A wild mustang was spotted in the desert.	(C)
FOREST	Robin Hood lived in Sherwood Forest.	(P)
	The scouts camped in the forest.	(C)

READ-OUT FOR NOUNS

OBJECTIVES: To improve usage and understanding of nouns.
To improve usage and understanding of common/proper nouns.
To improve usage and understanding of plurals.
To improve auditory memory skills.

TARGET POPULATION: Grades 2-5

MATERIALS: One basal reader per student

PROCEDURE: Choose a story from the reading text that students have already read. Inform the class of the pages that will pertain to this activity and have students mark these pages.

Choose a noun category, such as "plural common noun", from the provided list and read it aloud. Students individually search the designated pages of their texts for a plural common noun. There will probably be several examples within those pages. As each student finds a word that fulfills the stated category, she places her finger on the word and raises her hand.

When about half of the students are ready to respond, call on one child. She must tell the page number where her word was found, and then state the word that she believes fulfills the given category. All other students should turn to the same page and follow along as the student reads the entire sentence which contains the plural common noun. After the sentence has been read, ask if anyone has found a different word that fits the same category. Follow the same procedure, allowing two or three children to respond to each category. New answers may be either a different noun that fits the category, or a different sentence with the same noun.

Choose another noun category and announce it. Use the same pages previously used, or specify new pages for this category. The activity continues in this manner until time expires, or until everyone has responded at least once.

MODIFICATIONS: When a student has found a noun that she thinks fits the designated category, ask her to read the sentence without revealing her selected noun. Then ask another student to choose the correct noun from that sentence, if indeed there was one.

This activity can be played in teams with points awarded for correctly identifying appropriate nouns. Additional points may be given for reading the sentence correctly from beginning to end.

Categories

PROPER SINGULAR NOUN (Jaclyn)
COMMON SINGULAR NOUN (couch)
COMMON PLURAL NOUN (cribs)
PROPER PLURAL NOUN (Catholics)

(It may difficult to find proper plural nouns in the reading text.)

Optional requirements: person(s), place(s), thing(s)

NOUN STORYTELLING

OBJECTIVES: To improve usage and understanding of nouns.
To improve vocabulary skills.
To improve auditory memory skills.
To communicate effectively.

TARGET POPULATION: Grades 1-5

MATERIALS: Person/Place/Thing list (provided)
Optional drawings of nouns (works well for lower grades)

PROCEDURE: Give each student three nouns: one person, one place, and one thing. (In primary grades picture cards may be used along with written words.) The three nouns are not to be shown to other students.

Tell each child that she is to make up a sentence or a brief story using all three nouns. Give all students a few minutes to plan their sentences/stories. When most students are ready, choose one to tell her story aloud. The other students must try to guess which were the designated nouns. They must identify each as a person, place or thing. If the storyteller adds a few extra details, she may be able to stump her classmates, but if she keeps the story basic, the others will usually be able to tell which nouns she was given.

Allow each child to have a turn being storyteller.

MODIFICATIONS: In upper grades the class may be divided into two teams. A player from the first team would tell her story to the other team, adding extra nouns to try to confuse them. Members of the second team would then try to identify the specified nouns. Points could be awarded for guessing correct nouns. Stories should be limited to three sentences.

The game can become more challenging if intentionally incongruent words, for example, "island", "Santa Claus" and "kangaroo" are listed together. The stories may be a little longer with the target nouns being harder to identify.

Person/Place/Thing List

castle	island	desert	school	mall	ranch
prince	Joe	Juan	cook	guard	cowboy
rubies	shoe	cactus	pizza	glass	saddle
circus	hospital	farm	park	ballgame	restaurant
janitor	sailor	writer	farmer	chef	referee
marker	basket	flowers	lamp	chair	monkey
factory	highway	barn	courthouse	basement	campground
manager	nurse	teacher	prisoner	secretary	maid
zipper	feather	nails	newspaper	mug	helmet
field	garden	playground	porch	theater	church
preacher	winner	adults	doctor	guard	husband
hat	arrow	alarm	dictionary	socks	hammer

100 NOUNS

OBJECTIVES: To improve usage and understanding of nouns.
To improve usage and understanding of synonyms.
To improve vocabulary skills.
To improve creative thinking.

TARGET POPULATION: Grades 1-4

MATERIALS: Sentence list (provided)
Chalkboard and chalk *or*
Chart paper and markers

PROCEDURE: Read a sentence from the provided list to the class and, if desired, write it on the chalkboard. Ask for volunteers to name one noun that could meaningfully complete that sentence. When a correct noun is named write it on the chalkboard or on chart paper. Continue to ask for meaningful responses for that sentence until ten appropriate nouns have been identified and listed. Once a noun has been written on the chart, it may not be used again for the remainder of the activity.

This activity provides a good opportunity to develop synonyms. When a child responds with a noun that has already been used, ask if she can think of another word that means about the same thing. After ten nouns have been written for a given sentence, start the next group of ten nouns using the next sentence. Conclude when you have written one hundred nouns on the chart.

MODIFICATIONS: In the upper grade levels, the class can be divided into two to four teams. Challenge each team to develop its own list for a given sentence. After a few minutes, compare lists aloud. Points can be awarded for each appropriate noun that no other team has suggested.

In a similar way lists of verbs, adjectives. . . can be developed by choosing appropriate sentences.

Sentence List

At the zoo we saw _____.
On her feet she wore _____.
Last week I rode in a(n) _____.
In the city Jake heard _____.
At the beach we found some _____.
Jeff read a great book about _____.
We can play in the_____.
Jackson threw a(n) _____.
Everyone knows how to use a(n) _____.
Put your paper in the _____.

For my birthday I got a(n) _____.
Uncle Ernie ate a whole _____.
The yard is filled with _____.
Grandmom planted some _____.
At the parade I saw _____.
Carla loves red _____.
Travis bought a new _____.
My parents always read _____.
On her face Sandra has a(n) _____.
Today they will visit their _____.

LAST LETTER - NEW NOUN

OBJECTIVES: To improve usage and understanding of nouns.
To improve auditory memory skills.

TARGET POPULATION: Grades 2-5

MATERIALS: None

PROCEDURE: Choose a student and ask him to name a singular noun. If, for example, the student says "sailor", the next student must use the last letter of the first student's noun and name a new noun that begins with that letter. The second student's answer could be "raisin". The next student's noun must begin with the last letter in "raisin", so a correct response could be "necklace".

The activity continues until each person in the classroom has had at least one turn to respond. No noun may be repeated during the exercise.

MODIFICATIONS: For younger students provide help as needed to ensure correct spelling. The words could be written on the chalkboard as the activity progresses.

This game can be played with verbs, geographical locations, thematic words... or with no specific category. The emphasis in a no-category game could be on spelling the words correctly.

The activity can be played as "last sound-new noun". This will prevent having to come up with a lot of words that begin with the letter "e". A response that could follow the word "necklace", for example, could be "song", since the "s" sound is actually the last sound heard in "necklace". Playing this way may improve sound discrimination skills in students.

🗀 ♈ ❄

NOUN TIC TAC TOE

OBJECTIVES: To improve usage and understanding of nouns.
To improve usage and understanding of common nouns.
To improve usage and understanding of proper nouns.
To improve strategies for success.
To improve analytical thinking.
To improve the ability to construct grammatically correct, logical sentences.

TARGET POPULATION: Grades 1-3

MATERIALS: Chalkboard and chalk

PROCEDURE: Divide the class into two groups, Team "X" and Team "O". On the chalkboard draw a 3 x 3 grid for a Tic Tac Toe game. Label each of the nine boxes of the grid with a type of noun such as common person, proper person, common place, proper place, common thing or proper thing.

One person from Team "X" comes to the board and chooses the space where she would like to place her team's mark. She reads aloud the label in that box and then names an appropriate noun. For example, a "proper place" could be "Washington". She then uses that noun in a sentence. If the sentence is done correctly, she may enter her team's mark in the selected space. Play then passes to the other team. If the student responds incorrectly, she receives no mark for her team and play passes to the other team. Be sure that every team member has had the opportunity to respond once before anyone gets a second turn. The first team to place three of its marks in a row wins the game.

MODIFICATIONS: The labels could be written on cards and passed out ahead of time to allow students time to plan ahead, or one card could be handed to each student as she comes forward to take her turn. This eliminates having to write the labels in each box on the chalkboard every time a new Tic Tac Toe grid is made.

Some texts include "animal" as a separate category of nouns. If appropriate, include common/proper animals as labels.

A 4 x 4 grid can be used to extend the game board. The team with four in a row or a mark in each corner is the winner.

PLURALITY

OBJECTIVES: To improve usage and understanding of plurals.
To improve vocabulary skills.
To improve independent decision making.
To improve listening skills.

TARGET POPULATION: Grades 2-5

MATERIALS: Noun list (provided)
1 smiley face card and 1 sad face card per student-copy from appendix
Chalkboard and chalk

PROCEDURE: Write the numbers 1-50 on the chalkboard. Choose a student and ask him to select a number from 1-50. Cross the number he selects off the chalkboard so that no one else may choose it. Read the noun that is assigned to the chosen number on the provided list. Ask the same student to say what the plural form of the noun would be if it were formed by adding only an "s" or "es". For example, if the noun is "child", the student should respond with "childs". That student then thinks of a sentence for his new plural noun and tells it to the class. ("The childs went to the circus.")

All students will then individually decide if "childs" is the correct plural form of "child". Each student who thinks the plural form was correct will prepare to hold up his smiley face card. Each student who thinks the form was incorrect will prepare to hold up his sad face card. Students should avoid letting other students know which card they have selected. This can be accomplished by placing the selected card on top of the other card and then holding both together against the chest.

When all students are ready say, "Raise your cards", and all students should do so simultaneously. No student may change his response after viewing the responses of others. It is now possible to see which students are having difficulty with plurals.

Inform students of the correct answer card, and the correct plural form. Restate the sentence with the appropriate plural form.

Continue play by choosing another student to select a number from 1-50, and proceed as above.

MODIFICATIONS: This activity can be done in a game format by dividing the class into teams with equal numbers of players. When responding, individuals with correct answers score one point each for their teams.

Noun List

1. dress
2. boy
3. bench
4. waitress
5. child
6. monkey
7. chief
8. gas
9. wish
10. paper
11. wife
12. book
13. foot
14. radio
15. bridge
16. carpet
17. chair
18. tax
19. goose
20. prince
21. cash
22. calf
23. tomato
24. witch
25. life
26. table
27. apartment
28. shoe
29. fox
30. suitcase
31. girl
32. leaf
33. letter
34. hallway
35. woman
36. bag
37. potato
38. thief
39. house
40. mouse
41. shirt
42. gift
43. shelf
44. moose
45. tooth
46. man
47. knife
48. cage
49. card
50. ox

(Add "s" or "es" to underlined words to form plurals.)

IN-TENSE VERBS

OBJECTIVES:
To improve usage and understanding of verbs.
To improve usage and understanding of verb tenses.
To improve vocabulary skills.
To improve teamwork and cooperation.
To improve strategies for success.
To improve creative thinking.

TARGET POPULATION: Grades 1-5

MATERIALS: Sentence list (provided)
Pencil and paper for each team
Chalkboard and chalk

PROCEDURE: Divide the class into teams. Give a pencil and paper to each team's designated recorder. Then write a sentence from the provided list on the board. Tell each team to record ten verbs that could logically fit into the sentence, but inform them specifically what verb tense they must use: simple past tense, simple present tense, or simple future tense.

After all groups have written ten verbs, ask team #1 to state its list. If any other team has any of those same ten verbs, they and team #1 must cross them off their lists. Then ask each of the other teams to reveal its remaining list, each time having duplicated verbs crossed off of all lists. Teams must also cross off verbs that are illogical or something other than the specified tense.

When all answers have been revealed, ask recorders to count the number of verbs that remain on their lists. Score one point for each.

When all points have been recorded for the first sentence, write a new sentence on the board. Instruct teams to begin a new list of ten verbs, reminding them not to repeat any previously used verbs. Tell students the verb tense that they are to use in the new sentence. Remind them that even though the tense has been changed, no verbs may be reused. For example, if "went" was previously used in a past tense sentence, "will go" may not be used in the future tense of another sentence because both are forms of the verb "go".

Continue the activity as described and score all points. Repeat as often as time allows and then total all points. The team with the most points at the end of play is the winner.

MODIFICATIONS: Adjust the tense requirement to suit the curriculum.

Sentence List

The flowers in the garden ________.
The bird ________ around the tree.
Brenda and Ben ________ for hours.
Everyone ________ in the gym.
Gavin ________ through the woods.
He ________ for ten minutes.
Samantha ________ at home.

Justin ________ the newspaper.
I ________ Mason and Dillon.
Megan ________ the dog.
Shelly ________ all of the food.
Dad ________ the table.
Audrey ________ the horse.
I ______ the sandwich.

TENSE UP

OBJECTIVES: To improve usage and understanding of verb tenses.
To improve vocabulary skills.
To increase the ability to construct grammatically correct, logical sentences.

TARGET POPULATION: Grades 2-5

MATERIALS: Verb cards-copy from appendix
Tense cards-copy from appendix

PROCEDURE: Shuffle the verb cards and place them face down in a pile. Do the same with the tense cards.

Divide the class into teams and ask one person from each team to draw one card from each pile. Each cardholder then shows his cards to his teammates. The cardholders may "try out" some potentially correct sentences on their teammates who are not permitted to speak, but who may shake their heads to indicate their approval or disapproval of a particular sentence. Correct sentences are those in which the selected verb is correctly used in the tense indicated on the tense card. Each cardholder continues to "try out" sentences until his teammates approve one.

When all cardholders are ready, ask each to reveal his selected cards to the class and to state his sentence. If the sentence is correct, his team scores a point.

The next player from each team then draws a card from each of the two piles and play continues as described. Continue the activity until every student has been a cardholder. The team with the most points at the end of the session is the winner.

MODIFICATIONS: Award an extra point to cardholders who produce a correct sentence that does not begin with the word "I".

❄ ✋ ❖ ✍ ♈ 🏳

TROUBLED BY IRREGULARITY?

OBJECTIVES: To improve usage and understanding of verb tenses.
To develop teamwork and cooperation.
To improve strategies for success.
To improve creative thinking.
To improve vocabulary skills.
To increase the ability to construct grammatically correct, logical sentences.

TARGET POPULATION: Grades 3-5

MATERIALS: Sentence list (provided)
Paper and pencil for each team
Chalkboard and chalk

PROCEDURE: Divide the class into teams and designate one member of each team to be recorder. Read to the class a sentence from the provided sentence list. Each sentence contains a blank for the insertion of one past tense verb. Each team discusses and selects a past tense verb that would meaningfully fit into the blank. The recorder writes the group's choice.

When all teams are ready points are scored as follows: No points are awarded for using an incorrect verb form or a verb that does not make sense in the sentence. One point is earned for correctly using a *regular* past tense verb. Two points are earned for correctly using an *irregular* past tense verb, but *if no other team uses that same irregular verb*, award three points.

Have each recorder state his team's sentence. Write on the chalkboard all verbs that were correctly used so that they will not be reused in future sentences. List the verbs on the board under the categories "Regular Verbs" and "Irregular Verbs".

Continue with the next sentence, following the same procedure. The team with the most points at the end of the session is the winner.

MODIFICATIONS: This activity can be done without using teams or scoring points. Read a sentence and ask the class to volunteer correct responses. Keep a tally that shows the number of regular vs. the number of irregular past tense verbs used.

This activity could be adapted for use with any other verb tense.

Sentence List

I ______ my car.
Bob ______ a message.
Dad ______ a puppy.
I ______ to the store.
Mary ______ with David.
Lisa ______ all night long.
She ______ the book.
I ______ better than you.
Sarah ______ the ball.
The doctor ______ me the medicine.

Sue ______ a movie.
Her dog ______ her cat.
He ______ you a picture.
Who ______ that cake?
They ______ the game on TV.
Dan ______ a gun.
Mr. Smith ______ me home.
John ______ his homework.
Jeff ______ like an animal.
I ______ a list of names.

WHAT CAN IT DO?

OBJECTIVES: To improve usage and understanding of verbs.
To improve usage and understanding of nouns.
To improve vocabulary skills.
To improve strategies for success.
To improve teamwork and cooperation.

TARGET POPULATION: Grades 1-5

MATERIALS: Noun list (provided)
Pencil and paper for each team
Chalkboard and chalk

PROCEDURE: Divide the class into teams. Select a recorder for each team and provide him with a piece of paper and a pencil. Write one noun from the provided list on the chalkboard. Tell teams to write five verbs (five actions) that the chosen noun could do. Before beginning practice a few examples so that students understand that they must write verbs that the noun could do, not verbs that could be done to the noun. For example, for "food", acceptable answers would include "smell", "spoil", "rot", "cost" and "burn". "Eat" would not be acceptable. Students should practice creativity in their selection of verbs because points will be awarded for *unduplicated* answers only.

When all teams have written five verbs, begin checking for unduplicated correct responses. If, for example, the chosen noun is "dog", acceptable answers would include "run", "eat", "jump", "swim" and "roll". If another team also chooses "swim" and "run", then neither of those teams will receive points for those two verbs. In that case, instruct teams to cross "swim" and "run" from their lists. When all teams' answers have been reported, ask teams to count how many of their five verbs have <u>not</u> been crossed off due to duplication or incorrectness, and award one point to the appropriate teams for each of their remaining verbs.

Instruct students that they may not reuse any previously used verbs for the rest of the activity.

Give students another noun and wait for teams to list five new verbs. Continue as described for as long as time permits.

When finished, tally all scores. The team with the most points is declared the winner.

MODIFICATIONS: Save the list of verbs that are generated from this activity as a word bank for use in future creative writing assignments.

Noun List

dog	car	radio	rain	toy	snow
raft	ball	teacher	water	fingers	bell
gun	maid	bird	medicine	oven	TV
army	fire	river	sun	horse	forest
witch	flower	mixer	machine	food	chef

ARE YOU REGULAR?

OBJECTIVES: To improve usage and understanding of verb tenses.
To improve independent decision making.
To improve listening skills.

TARGET POPULATION: Grades 2-5

MATERIALS: Verb list (provided)
Chalkboard and chalk
Smiley face cards and sad face cards-copy one per student from appendix

PROCEDURE: Write the numbers 1-49 on the chalkboard. Choose one student and ask him to select one of the numbers. Erase his selection from the board so that no one else may choose it. From the provided verb list read the present tense verb that is next to the student's number choice. Ask the student to say what the past tense form of the verb would be *if* it were a *regular* past tense verb. For example, if the present tense form is "eat", the student should respond with "eated". The same student then thinks of a sentence for his new past tense verb, such as "He eated his lunch", and tells it to the class.

All students will then individually decide if "eated" is the correct past tense form of "eat". Each student who thinks the past tense form is correct will prepare to hold up his smiley face card. Each student who thinks the form is incorrect will prepare to hold up his sad face card. Students should avoid letting other students know which card they have selected. This can be accomplished by placing the selected card on top of the other card and then holding both together against the chest.

When all students are ready say, "Raise your cards", and all students should do so simultaneously. No student may change his response after viewing the responses of others. It is now possible to see which students are having difficulty with past tense verbs. Inform students of the correct answer card and the correct past tense form of the given verb.

Continue play as above by choosing another student to select a number from the board.

MODIFICATIONS: This activity can be done in a game format by dividing the class into teams with equal numbers of players. When responding, individuals with correct answers score a point for their teams.

Verb List

1. spray	8. wear	15. cost	22. come	29. earn	36. draw	43. put
2. pick	9. kill	16. ask	23. ring	30. leave	37. win	44. dig
3. lose	10. eat	17. croak	24. have	31. climb	38. sell	45. stack
4. sing	11. talk	18. lock	25. answer	32. reach	39. count	46. stay
5. swing	12. bend	19. clean	26. know	33. trick	40. grow	47. say
6. whisper	13. roar	20. want	27. follow	34. watch	41. listen	48. get
7. mail	14. cheat	21. deal	28. blow	35. peel	42. think	49. chase

(Irregular verbs are underlined.)

BATTER UP!

OBJECTIVES:
To improve usage and understanding of verbs.
To improve usage and understanding of verb tenses.
To improve usage and understanding of subjects.
To improve usage and understanding of proper nouns.
To improve usage and understanding of pronouns.
To improve usage and understanding of plurals.
To improve following direction skills.
To increase the ability to construct grammatically correct, logical sentences.

TARGET POPULATION: Grades 3-5

MATERIALS: Subject/verb cards-
copy from appendix
Chalkboard and chalk
2 different magnets *or*
2 differently marked self-stick notes

TIME: Allow 45 minutes

PROCEDURE: Divide the class into two teams. Students may remain in their seats or be seated on the floor in two lines near the chalkboard.

Draw a simple baseball diamond on the chalkboard (see illustration below). Use the 2 magnets or self-stick notes to represent the two teams. Place both markers at "home". Alternate play between teams with one player "batting" at a time. The teacher functions as both the pitcher and the umpire.

The first player "at bat" randomly selects one of the subject/verb cards and reads it aloud. Each card specifies three components: 1) noun or pronoun subject; 2) singular or plural subject; and 3) past, present or future tense verb. The "batter" must state a sentence which includes the indicated components in a grammatically correct, meaningful sentence.

For example, if the card states "subject = singular noun, verb = past tense" a correct response would include "The army truck rolled down the highway." For each of the three required components that is correct, advance the team's marker one base. Every time the marker reaches home plate the team scores a run.

Play continues until every student has been "at bat" at least one time.

MODIFICATIONS: The "balls" (subject/verb cards) could be "pitched" to each player ahead of time to allow ample time to prepare sentences. Each student may then write her sentence on paper to make it easier to remember when it is her turn to respond.

This activity could be modified to suit your curriculum by specifying components other than those listed above, such as parts of speech.

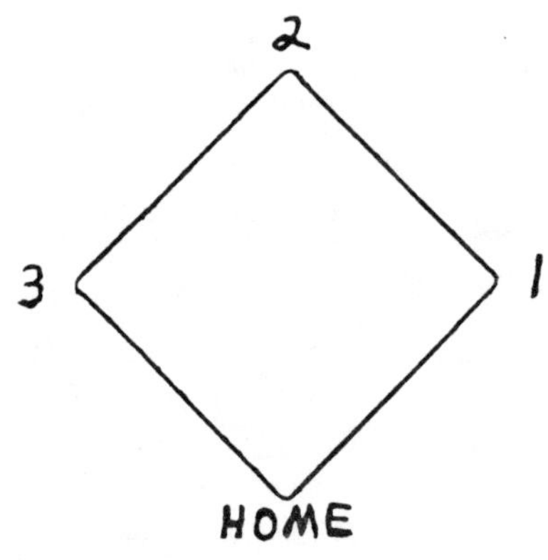

SENTENCE TIC TAC TOE

OBJECTIVES: To improve usage and understanding of verbs.
To improve usage and understanding of nouns.
To improve strategies for success.
To improve vocabulary skills.
To increase the ability to construct grammatically correct, logical sentences.

TARGET POPULATION: Grades 1-5

MATERIALS: Chalkboard and chalk

PROCEDURE: On the chalkboard draw a simple 4 x 4 grid as in the illustration below. (A 5 x 5 grid could also be used.) Print four nouns across the top of the grid, one above each of the four spaces. Print four verbs to the left of the grid, one beside each space.

Divide the class into two teams. Designate one team as "X" and the other as "O". Teams will take turns trying to win squares on the grid. The first team to complete a horizontal, vertical or diagonal line with its symbols wins the game.

The first player chooses the square that she would like to win. Teammates are not permitted to instruct the player as to which square to choose for a specific strategy. The player herself must make that decision.

To win that particular square a player must use two specific words, the noun above the column and the verb beside the row, in a grammatically correct, meaningful sentence. For example, if the two words are "clock" and "hug", a correct sentence would be "Mom will hug me when the clock strikes one." An inappropriate response would be "The clock will hug me." Players must also take care to use the noun as a noun and the verb as a verb.

After a sentence is stated, allow the other team to decide if it was correct. If a player does not make a correct sentence, she cannot mark a square. When a player does earn a square by correctly producing a sentence, she puts her team's mark in the corresponding space. Correct or not, play then passes to the other team.

Word forms may be changed to accommodate verb format. "Jump", for example, may be changed to "jumped" or "jumping". Singular nouns may also be changed to plural.

If neither team completes four squares in a row, there is no winner.

MODIFICATIONS: To make this more challenging for upper grades, the same words can be used across and down the grid. For example, words like "party", "box", and "race" can be used as both verbs and nouns.

This game format can also be adapted for other parts of speech, such as adjectives/nouns, adverbs/verbs, etc.

	clock	garage	school	uncle
hug				
kick				
smile				
write				

VERB BEE

OBJECTIVES:
- To improve usage and understanding of verbs.
- To improve vocabulary skills.
- To improve auditory memory.
- To improve usage and understanding of synonyms.
- To improve creative thinking.
- To increase the ability to construct grammatically correct, logical sentences.

TARGET POPULATION: Grades 2-5

MATERIALS: Sentence list (provided)
Chalkboard and chalk

PROCEDURE: Divide the class into two teams. Have teams line up on opposite sides of the room facing each other. Read aloud a sentence from the provided list. The first person from team one repeats the sentence, inserting into the blank a verb that would correctly complete it. In the example, "A mouse _____ across the floor" an acceptable response would be "The mouse scurried across the floor." If the suggested word creates a grammatically correct, meaningful sentence, the student remains standing. If a student suggests an inappropriate, ungrammatical, or previously used verb, she must sit down for the remainder of the game.

Play then passes to the other team and the first player on that team states aloud the *same* sentence, but inserts a different verb. "The mouse ran across the floor" would be another correct response. Once a verb has been used, it may not be used again during the activity. Elicit at least 8-10 different verbs before moving on to a new sentence. Students will thus be encouraged to come up with synonyms of previously used verbs.

The team with the most players standing at the end of time is declared the winner.

MODIFICATIONS: This activity can be played as a "circle bee" with all students standing in a large circle. Begin by asking everyone wearing blue jeans (or black shoes, or pants with pockets...) to sit in her place on the circle. The first round is played using one sentence. Each standing student must supply a verb to complete a grammatically correct sentence, or sit down. Then before presenting the new sentence, ask all students who are standing to sit and all who are sitting to stand. Continue the activity, switching participants after each round.

In grades 3-5 this activity can be done in teams of four or five students who work together to compile a list of verbs to complete a given sentence. After a specified amount of time, points are awarded for each correct verb that *no other team has* on its list.

Sentence List

The mouse ________ across the floor.
The clown ________ the baby elephant.
The sailor ________ the huge ship.
The nurse ________ her patient.
Helen and I ________ the house.
Mom ________ the flowers in the house.
We ________ until one o'clock in the morning.
Ms. Nelson ________ her hair.
My dad ________ his new red truck.
The cowboy ________ through the desert.
Sammy ________ six hot dogs.
The kids ________ their math books.
Marvin ________ around the park.
My brother ________ the orange ball.
Grandpop ________ the baby.
The guys ________ when they saw him.

VERB DETECTIVE

OBJECTIVES:
- To improve usage and understanding of verbs.
- To improve vocabulary skills.
- To improve strategies that bring success.
- To improve auditory memory skills.
- To improve listening skills.
- To improve independent decision making.
- To improve analytical thinking.

TARGET POPULATION: Grades 2-5

MATERIALS: Sentence list (provided)
Pencil and paper for each student

PROCEDURE: Divide students into teams. Provide each student with a piece of paper and a pencil. Explain that students will be writing down one, *and only one*, verb from the sentence that will be read. If teams cannot be divided evenly, it will be necessary to declare someone from each of the "shorted" teams to be the "double respondent". This person can write two verbs for each sentence, or teammates can take turns being the "double respondent". This ensures that all teams are given an equal number of responses per sentence.

Read a sentence from the provided list three times so that no one must ask for repetition. Explain that team points will be kept and that points will be earned as follows: If a student writes a word that is actually used as a verb in the given sentence, *and no more than three students from the class have chosen that same verb*, each of the students who has written that verb scores one point for his team. It is possible that all of the points may go to the same team. Explain to students that it is to their advantage to choose a verb that they think few others will choose. Copying a verb that someone else has written will decrease the chances of scoring points.

After reading the sentence three times, and when all students are ready with one written verb, begin checking responses. Read the sentence with a pause between each word. When the student hears the teacher say the word that he has written, he must immediately raise his hand or be left out of the count. Tally each point as it is earned. Be sure to inform students which words are verbs in the sentence even if no one has selected a particular verb. Also explain why incorrect responses are not verbs in that sentence.

Continue by reading the next sentence three times and following the same procedure. The team with the most points at the end of the session is declared the winner.

MODIFICATIONS: Consider deducting a point from a team if one of its members writes a word that is not used as a verb in the given sentence.

VERB DETECTIVE

Sentence List

John drove to the store, bought the groceries, brought them home, and put them away.

The teacher noticed that everyone in the class drew a picture, cut it out, and taped it to the wall.

My brother came home, took a shower, brushed his teeth, and went back out.

After you clean the garage and pick up the junk, please take the trash to the dump and burn it.

As the crook moved, the police officer yelled, "If you run, I shoot".

Each Sunday we go to church, eat dinner, and change our clothes before we start any other activity.

Exercise, eat right, watch your weight, and live a long time.

When the movie started, our dog bit our cat, Jeffrey caught the dog, and Dad put both animals in their pens.

I love pizza and I crave hamburgers, but I prepared spaghetti tonight because we invited special guests for dinner.

The doctor examined the patient, read her medical report, conferred with some specialists, and then made a recommendation.

The puppies jumped and squealed when they saw Ben open the door.

Sally wanted a bike for Christmas and Jack hoped and prayed for a trampoline, but both of them enjoyed what they got.

They saw the man who hit and killed the deer, and then drove off.

The people screamed and cheered when the band came out on the stage and played everyone's favorite song.

If you fix breakfast, please clean up your mess and wash the dishes before you leave.

The fireman said that the fire started in the kitchen, ignited some curtains, spread down the hallway, and destroyed the entire house.

While you sit here and watch TV, please fold these towels and sort the socks for me.

Gavin wanted tacos for dinner so he diced some tomatoes, shredded some cheese, broke up some lettuce, and cooked the ground beef.

Mom bought a stereo, but when it broke, she called the store manager and complained.

Please clap if you like the performance or sit quietly if you dislike it.

VERB TICKETS

OBJECTIVES:
- To improve usage and understanding of verbs.
- To improve usage and understanding of adverbs.
- To improve vocabulary skills.
- To improve strategies for success.
- To improve analytical thinking.
- To increase the ability to communicate effectively.

TARGET POPULATION: Grades 3-5

MATERIALS: Verb list (provided)
3 tickets per team-copy from appendix

PROCEDURE: Divide students into three teams. Select one person from each team to be the ticket holder for the first round of play. Each ticket holder is given three tickets and sent out of hearing distance, such as in the hallway. Select a verb from the provided list and reveal it to the remaining students. Then instruct the ticket holders to return to the classroom.

Ask non-ticket holders to raise their hands when they can think of an adverb that could be used to modify the secret verb. Select any student and ask him to state his adverb.

After hearing the first clue, the first ticket holder, *if any*, to raise his hand has the opportunity to guess the secret verb. His guess will cost him one of his verb tickets. When a ticket holder spends all three of his tickets, he may no longer guess. If the ticket holder guesses the verb correctly, he scores one point for his team. If he was incorrect, any of the other ticket holders may spend one of his tickets and take a guess. When no ticket holder wishes to continue guessing from that particular clue, select another student to provide an additional adverb that could be used to describe the same verb. Remind students to consider both adverbs already given when trying to come up with the correct verb. Again the first ticket holder to raise his hand may spend a ticket and guess. Play on this verb continues until a ticket holder is correct, all tickets have been spent, or it is decided that too much time has been spent on that particular verb. If any non-ticket holder who is selected to provide an adverb actually states something other than an adverb, or uses more than one word, his ticket-holding teammate is not permitted to guess from that clue.

Round two begins by selecting new ticket holders from each group, sending then out of the room and revealing a new verb to the remaining classmates. Play continues at least until every student has had the opportunity to be a ticket holder. The team with the most points at the end of the session is the winner.

MODIFICATIONS: Write student-provided adverbs on the chalkboard or on chart paper as a word bank for use in future writing assignments.

Verb List

eat	sing	run	write	yell	cry	fight
steal	kill	win	fall	hold	drive	fly
cook	grow	break	think	draw	concentrate	shop
act	play	turn	pray	work	listen	swim
smell	taste	touch	cheat	stand	tie	wait
push	fix	build	ask	paint	swing	talk

CONTRACTION ACTION

OBJECTIVES: To improve usage and understanding of contractions.
To improve teamwork and cooperation.
To improve vocabulary skills.

TARGET POPULATION: Grades 2-5

MATERIALS: Word cards-copy from appendix
Contraction list-see appendix
Tape
Chalkboard and chalk
Whistle (optional)

PROCEDURE: Shuffle the deck of word cards and deal one card to each student. The deck may be "stacked" so that students who are having difficulty with contractions are given cards which contain words that are more often contracted, such as "is" or "not". Each student reads his word and then tapes it to his shirt or to his forehead so that others can easily read it. Instruct students to simultaneously roam the room in search of other students who have cards containing words which can be combined with their own to form contractions. When a pair of students thinks that a contraction can be formed from their words, the two lock arms and raise their free hands. When several pairs are ready to respond, blow your whistle or call, "Freeze". All students must silently "freeze" in their tracks and listen. Select one pair and point to the person who has the first word of the contraction. He says his word aloud. Then point to his partner who says his word aloud. Finally point to both of them, and they say their contraction in unison. Write the contraction on the chalkboard. Repeat this procedure with all other pairs who are ready to respond. When all have finished say "Resume", and all students, including those whose contractions have already been used, continue to search for new partners.

When students can find no more contractions, ask one student to come to the chalkboard and point out each contraction that was formed with his word. This provides a quick review and allows students to see that some words are contracted more often than others. When this student has finished, challenge classmates to name additional contractions that were omitted. Write those on the board as well.

Call the next student to the chalkboard and repeat this process. Conclude the activity when all have finished this task.

Check the appendix for a list of contractions that can be formed from the words on the provided word cards. Inform students if there are additional contractions that they have missed and write them on the board.

MODIFICATIONS:

NOUN, PRONOUN, NEITHER

OBJECTIVES:
To improve usage and understanding of nouns.
To improve usage and understanding of pronouns.
To improve independent decision making.
To improve listening skills.
To improve auditory memory skills.

TARGET POPULATION: Grades 2-5

MATERIALS: Sentence list (provided)
#1. #2 and #3 cards-copy one per student from appendix
Chalkboard and chalk

PROCEDURE: Give each student a #1 card, a #2 card and a #3 card. On the chalkboard write the following answer key for the number cards:

#1=NOUN   #2=PRONOUN   #3=NEITHER A NOUN NOR A PRONOUN

Instruct students that holding up a #1 card indicates that they have chosen "noun" as an answer, #2 means "pronoun", etc. Make sure that all students understand this correspondence by asking them to hold up the card that means "pronoun"... When students understand the correspondence, begin.

Tell the class the target word for the first sentence chosen from the provided list, and then read the sentence. Instruct students that they are to determine if the target word was used as a noun, pronoun or neither in the given sentence. For example, if the target word is "you", and the sentence is, "Don gave you the ball yesterday", students who understand the instructions and the concepts will prepare to hold up their #2 cards. Each student selects the # card of his choice and holds it against his chest to prevent others from viewing it. The # cards which he has not selected should be turned face down on his desk.

When all students are ready, say "Raise your cards", and all students should do so simultaneously. No student is permitted to change his selection at this point. It is now easy to identify those students who are having difficulty with the concepts of nouns and/or pronouns.

Continue the activity with another target word and sentence.

MODIFICATIONS: Before beginning the activity it would be beneficial to explain that words that are normally thought of as nouns are sometimes used as other parts of speech. For example, the word "chicken" is used as an adjective in the phrase "chicken dinner".

This activity may be played as a game if the class is divided into teams. Team points can be earned by individual members responding correctly, or by the spokesperson of the group being correct when reporting the consensus of the group. If individual players are earning points for their teams, be certain that all teams have an equal number of players.

NOUN, PRONOUN, NEITHER
Sentence List

they	They didn't know that we were coming.	(pronoun)
floor	Please help me clean up the floor.	(noun)
chicken	Mom fixed a great chicken dinner today.	(neither)
stomach	I have a pain in my stomach.	(noun)
flowers	The class sent her some flowers while she was in the hospital.	(noun)
us	Mrs. Jones wanted to give us a Christmas present.	(pronoun)
car	The car door has been jammed ever since the accident.	(neither)
clown	Audrey was the winner of the balloon that the clown made.	(noun)
children	All of the children returned their permission slips.	(noun)
guitar	When I'm older I'll be able to take guitar lessons.	(neither)
Halloween	The Halloween party will begin right after the parade.	(neither)
anybody	Does anybody know where I put my jacket?	(pronoun)
me	Myriah didn't leave me any mess to clean up.	(pronoun)
class	The class trip has been canceled due to bad weather.	(neither)
bell	When you hear the two o'clock bell meet me in the gym.	(noun)
table	Suzanne was responsible for all of the table decorations.	(neither)
everyone	Everyone at the festival was impressed with her crafts.	(pronoun)
string	You'll have to put a string around the top of that bag.	(noun)
swing	Clinton will swing until his mom comes to pick him up.	(neither)
rest	Dad wants to stop for a short rest.	(noun)
change	Barb will change her clothes before she leaves for practice.	(neither)
party	Jessica's mom bought her a beautiful white party dress.	(neither)
crowd	Everyday Pete and Brian crowd me out of the lunch line.	(neither)
it	After you finish your homework have your parents sign it.	(pronoun)
walk	The elderly people were having a nice walk through the park.	(noun)
cry	The cry of the wolf made all of the campers a little nervous.	(noun)
book	We have to have one book report ready by next week.	(neither)
calculator	Grandma is going to get new batteries for our calculator.	(noun)
neither	Neither of the boys made the basketball team.	(pronoun)
who	The police do not know who broke into the library.	(pronoun)

NOUN / PRONOUN SUBSTITUTION

OBJECTIVES: To improve usage and understanding of pronouns.
To improve usage and understanding of nouns.
To improve listening skills.
To improve auditory memory skills.

TARGET POPULATION: Grades 2-5

MATERIALS: Sentence list (provided)
Chalkboard and chalk

PROCEDURE: Have all students stand and form a circle around the room. Inform them that a sentence will be read aloud two times. After a "thinking minute", the students, in a particular order, will attempt to change the sentence by substituting a noun or noun phrase for the pronoun used, and a pronoun for the noun or noun phrase used. For example, if the sentence read was "My mother made it", a correct response would be "She made the dress." "She" is substituted for "my mother", and "the dress" for "it". "She made the cake" would also be a correct response. When replacing the pronouns "we" and "us", it is acceptable to use a noun plus the pronoun "I" or "me". "John and I", for example, could be substituted for "we".

After the "thinking minute" point to any student in the circle, pause, point to the next student in the circle, pause, point to the next student, pause... in a rotation around the circle until one student says, "stop". This is the student who is ready to give a response. If his response is correct, he sits down where he has been standing. If he is incorrect, he remains standing. Continue pointing to students around the circle until someone responds correctly.

If no one is correct after one entire loop around the circle, guide students to an appropriate response, and then put a tally mark on the chalkboard. The tally indicates that all students were stumped.

Read the next sentence twice. With this sentence begin by pointing at the student who is next in order after the last correct respondent. Point only to students who are still standing.

Continue the procedure until everyone is sitting. The goal is to have everyone sitting before there are more than three tally marks (or some other predetermined number) on the chalkboard.

If time allows, begin the activity again.

MODIFICATIONS: Have each respondent make only one substitution in the sentence with the next respondent making the second change.

If there are several students in the class who are having much difficulty with this activity, do not require that *everyone* be sitting before concluding, or play the game in partners with two students sitting or standing together.

Write sentences on the chalkboard to decrease the number of times they need to be repeated. This will also benefit visual learners.

NOUN / PRONOUN SUBSTITUTION
Sentence List

John brought it here earlier.
She almost sent the letter today.
The boys finally left it there.
He will not visit our class tomorrow.
They barely fed the dogs enough.
She anxiously answered the telephone.
David didn't sell them yesterday.
Someone forgot to finish the painting.
The Green Bay Packers easily won it.
It will be delivered by Andrea very soon.
Andrew signed up to bring something.
The tree was decorated yesterday by them.
We just decided to purchase a stereo.
They unanimously elected the president today.
After the girls eat, we will leave.
Somebody likes to read the newspaper daily.
We whole heartedly believe in angels.
They were very unfair to Tommy.
The maid remembered to wash them.
Hannah chased us all day.
The children really listened to them.
The computer was programmed by her.
The waitress brought it right away.
My great grandfather buried it over there.
He shaved his mustache off.
Dr. Morgan hoped to marry her soon.
The lights were pointed directly at them.
We listened to the music nonstop.
The photographer told us to smile.
A duck swam right past them.

(Underlined words must be substituted.)

PRONOUN DETECTIVE

OBJECTIVES:
To improve usage and understanding of pronouns.
To improve vocabulary skills.
To improve strategies for success.
To improve auditory memory skills.
To improve listening skills.
To improve independent decision making.
To improve analytical thinking.

TARGET POPULATION: Grades 2-5

MATERIALS: Sentence list (provided)
Paper and pencil for each student

PROCEDURE: Divide students into several teams. Provide each student with a piece of paper and a pencil. Explain that students will be writing down one, *and only one*, pronoun from the sentence that will be read. If teams cannot be divided evenly, it will be necessary to declare someone from each of the "shorted" teams to be the "double respondent". This person can write two pronouns for each sentence, or teammates can take turns being the "double respondent". This ensures that all teams are given an equal number of responses per sentence. Students will be working independently to score points for their teams.

Read a sentence from the provided list three times so that no one must ask for repetition. Explain that team points will be kept, and that points will be earned as follows: If a student writes a word that is actually used as a pronoun in the given sentence, *and no more than three students from the class have chosen that same pronoun,* each of the students who has written that pronoun scores one point for his team. It is possible that all of the points may go to the same team. Explain to students that it is to their advantage to choose a pronoun that they think few others will choose. Copying a pronoun that someone else has written will decrease the chances of scoring points.

After reading the sentence three times, and when all students are ready with one written pronoun, begin checking responses. Reread the sentence with a pause after each word. When the student hears the teacher say the word that he has written, he must immediately raise his hand or be left out of the count. Tally each point as it is earned. Be sure to inform students which words are pronouns in the sentence even if some were not chosen as responses. Also explain why incorrect responses are not pronouns in that sentence.

Continue by reading the next sentence three times and following the same procedure. The team with the most points at the end of the session is declared the winner.

MODIFICATIONS: Deduct a point from a team if one of its members writes a word that is not used as a pronoun in the given sentence.

Pronouns such as "everyone", "anything", "somebody"... may or may not be included in this lesson, but students generally learn them very quickly.

Students working in teams or individually try to identify *all* pronouns in a sentence.

PRONOUN DETECTIVE
Sentence List

When he has finished with her, we will tell him the news.
Everybody knows nothing would make her happier than that.
Martha and I told each of you something would happen to us today.
We don't know anything about anyone in fourth grade.
That was somebody at the door who wanted to sell us a book.
All of them thought it was a party for me.
Why can't I go with you to see everyone at the office?
He told them we would be back before anyone missed us.
Who told you about all of the work we have done?
Each of them found someone to do it.
Neither of us told her to stay in bed and do nothing.
Some say we will have a snowstorm if it stays this cold.
Why didn't you tell us something about that?
She couldn't wait to tell everyone about the ring he gave her.
We can choose either of the boys to be captain if it is alright with you.
All of them knew a little something about how it had happened.
Any of us could be someone who needs a heart transplant.
This is why both of you should be prepared to help her.
Why would they trust you when we know that is a lie?
Did anyone say anything to you about them?
I hope you won't tell her anything about it.
She and I have nothing to say to you.
They told us everything we wanted to know.
He gave her and me something we will never forget.
Ask them to tell you everything they know about him.

(Underlined words are pronouns.)

I SPY A PRONOUN

OBJECTIVES: To improve usage and understanding of pronouns.
To improve independent decision making.
To improve listening skills.
To improve analytical thinking.

TARGET POPULATION: Grades 2-5

MATERIALS: Sentence list (provided)
Smiley face and sad face cards-copy one each per student from appendix

PROCEDURE: Give each student a smiley face card and a sad face card. Instruct students that they are to determine if a sentence that is read to them contains a pronoun. Emphasize that a pronoun is a person, place or thing that takes the place of a noun. This would include such words as "someone", "everybody", "nothing", etc.

Choose a sentence from the sentence list and read it to the class twice. If a student determines that there is *at least one* pronoun in that sentence, he will prepare to hold up his smiley face card. If he thinks there are no pronouns, he will prepare to hold up his sad face card. Students do not raise the card of their choice until instructed to do so. They should avoid letting other students know which card they have chosen. This can be accomplished by placing the chosen card on top of the unselected one, and then holding both cards together against the chest. When all cards are against the chests, everyone is ready to respond. Say "Raise your cards." All students simultaneously do so with no one being permitted to alter his choice. By viewing the raised card of each student it is easy to identify which students are having difficulty understanding pronouns.

Tell students the pronoun(s) in the sentence, if any. Then ask someone to volunteer to tell what each of the pronouns could be referring to. For example, if "they" was used in the sentence, some possibilities for referrents might be "ten people", "some trees", "the Boy Scouts", "your neighbors", etc.

Continue by reading the next sentence and following the same procedure.

MODIFICATIONS: This activity may also be played as a game if the class is divided into teams. Team points can be earned by individual members responding correctly, or by the "spokesperson" of the group who correctly responds with the general consensus of the group. If individuals are earning points for their teams, be certain that all teams have equal numbers of players.

Pronouns such as "everyone", "anything", "somebody"... may or may not be included in this lesson, but students generally learn them very quickly.

I SPY A PRONOUN

Sentence List

If there is a question, <u>I</u> would be glad to help.
<u>We</u> are not allowed to write on the bathroom walls.
The teachers told stories to the interested students.
The kids complained that there was <u>nothing</u> to do.
Easter always falls on a Sunday.
Sally and <u>I</u> are going on vacation this summer.
The TV is too loud!
Bob will buy <u>something</u> for Mom's birthday.
A friend wrote a letter to the President of the United States.
Did <u>you</u> hear about the forest fires in California?
<u>Anything</u> Grandma brings for dinner will be fine.
The animals in the barn huddled together to keep warm.
When Dad got to the house, <u>he</u> called to say that Bill had also arrived.
Bridget painted the little girl's fingernails yesterday morning.
Mr. Braun had shiny stickers for <u>each</u> of <u>us</u>.
<u>Somebody</u> broke into the grocery store last month.
<u>Both</u> of the doctors agreed on the diagnosis.
Did the entire class understand <u>this</u>?
<u>Neither</u> of the new fathers knows how to change a diaper.
Marvin made a special hat for the celebration.
Mom is not sure what job <u>she</u> will have next year.
Ask <u>them</u> if the parents have left yet.
The sweeper bag broke and dust filled the room.
Dad gave money to <u>someone</u> at the office.
Unusual things happen at the county fair.
Do the boys know <u>anything</u> about the surprise party?
Pick up the cards and put <u>them</u> in a container.
Tommy couldn't believe <u>it</u> was finally Christmas.
Tell <u>him</u> to get the groceries out of the van.
<u>Some</u> say a red sky in the morning means bad weather is coming.
The newspaper reporter suggested how to write the article.
Did <u>they</u> say whether the pool would be open tonight?
<u>That</u> is totally ridiculous!
The alarm clock has two broken hands.
The Girl Scouts sold <u>all</u> of the cookies.
<u>Everybody</u> in the gym was singing during the concert.
Mark will give the tablet to <u>her</u> on the bus.

(Pronouns are underlined.)

GO TOGETHERS

OBJECTIVES:
- To improve usage and understanding of nouns.
- To improve usage and understanding of adjectives.
- To improve vocabulary skills.
- To improve creative thinking.
- To increase the ability to construct grammatically correct, logical sentences.

TARGET POPULATION: Grades 2-5

MATERIALS: Noun list (provided)
Adjective list (provided)
Paper and pencil for each student

PROCEDURE: Divide students into teams. Each student will work independently but will score points for his team. Ask each student to write two numbers from 1-50 on his paper. If he chooses, he may write the same number twice. The first number that the student writes will correspond to an adjective from the provided list. The second number will identify a noun from the noun list. When everyone is ready, inform each student of his two selected words. Students should write the words on paper to avoid forgetting them. It does not matter if several students choose the same number from either list, as long as both numbers are not the same. When everyone knows his adjective and noun, play begins.

Each student working independently attempts to produce a sentence in which his chosen adjective can be used to describe his chosen noun. Students should write their sentences so that they will not forget them while waiting to respond. When everyone has finished, or a specified amount of time has elapsed, ask one student at a time to state his adjective and noun, and to read the sentence that he has written. If a student has successfully created a sentence in which his adjective is used to describe his noun, he earns two points for his team. If a student cannot think of such a sentence he is still able to earn one point for his team by having written a single sentence which contains both of his selected words, even though the adjective does not describe the noun. For example, if the student's words are "fuzzy" and "book", the student can earn a single point by writing a sentence such as, "I sat down on my fuzzy red chair to read this wonderful book".

At times an explanation may be required from a student in order to determine if his sentence makes sense. For example, the student may write, "I read his fuzzy book to him." A first reaction might be that the sentence is illogical, but if the student explains that his baby brother has an animal book with a fuzzy cover, points should be awarded.

If time allows after all students have responded, let each select two more numbers and repeat the process. Do not allow a student to select the same adjective or noun that he has previously chosen. The team with the most points at the end of play is the winner.

MODIFICATIONS: When telling students the adjectives and the nouns that they have selected, do so quietly or show them the words by pointing to them on the list. Do not ask students to reveal their words before stating their sentences. After a sentence is read ask for volunteers to guess the adjective and the noun that the student was given.

Do the activity without awarding points.

GO TOGETHERS

Adjective List

1. fuzzy
2. crazy
3. delicious
4. unusual
5. nervous
6. older
7. gorgeous
8. slippery
9. fancy
10. nasty
11. narrow
12. perfect
13. special
14. striped
15. quiet
16. expensive
17. smelly
18. noisy
19. spotted
20. dusty
21. famous
22. colorful
23. sticky
24. better
25. dark
26. important
27. wooden
28. scary
29. interesting
30. long
31. amazing
32. excellent
33. gigantic
34. short
35. dull
36. bright
37. sweet
38. exciting
39. messy
40. crooked
41. rich
42. sour
43. hot
44. wet
45. stiff
46. dry
47. icy
48. lazy
49. tall
50. odd

Noun List

1. flowers
2. party
3. river
4. restaurant
5. wedding
6. breakfast
7. infant
8. friend
9. pyramid
10. animals
11. house
12. spaghetti
13. fingers
14. socks
15. noises
16. pictures
17. wallpaper
18. vehicle
19. raincoat
20. message
21. dessert
22. story
23. office
24. church
25. peach
26. woman
27. sidewalk
28. necklace
29. jewelry
30. movie
31. vacation
32. glasses
33. blanket
34. idea
35. food
36. evening
37. carpet
38. lesson
39. factory
40. teacher
41. hand
42. toys
43. fish
44. book
45. hair
46. time
47. cat
48. road
49. room
50. day

HEADLINE NEWS

OBJECTIVES: To improve usage and understanding of adjectives.
To improve creative thinking.
To improve auditory memory skills.
To improve strategies for success.
To improve independent decision making.

TARGET POPULATION: Grades 2-5

MATERIALS: Newspaper headlines- see appendix
Paper and pencil for each student

PROCEDURE: Show the class some samples of newspaper headlines, and discuss what kinds of words are missing. Point out that due to space restrictions, only a minimal amount of information can be included in headlines. Explain that inserting adjectives would result in much more interesting reading.

Read a headline to the class. Ask for volunteers to tell which nouns or pronouns could be described by an adjective. When a specific noun or pronoun has been identified, ask the class for suggestions of adjectives that could describe it. After several suggestions have been made, the activity begins.

Divide the class into teams. If teams cannot be evenly divided, designate one person from each of the "shorted" teams to be the "double respondent". This person will write two responses each time so that all teams have an equal opportunity to score points. Students can alternate being the "double respondent".

Seat teammates in rows. Students will be writing answers independently, but will be scoring points for their teams.

Read another headline to the class. Ask for a volunteer to tell one word in the headline which could use a descriptive adjective. Tell each student to write one adjective which could describe that word.

When all students have written one adjective, scoring begins. Ask each student, one at a time, to state the word that he has written. *If he is the only classmate who has written that word,* a point is scored for his team. Everyone will score a point if all answers are acceptable adjectives, and there are no repetitions.

Explain to students that once an adjective has been used, it may not be used again for the duration of the activity.

Ask students to name another noun or pronoun in that headline, or in a different headline, that could use an adjective. Allow everyone time to write his next adjective to describe the newly chosen word. Award points for acceptable unduplicated responses.

Continue with additional headlines. The team with the most points at the end of the activity is declared the winner.

MODIFICATIONS: ❄ ✋ ❖ 🗀 ♈ ✍

ONE DESCRIBES BOTH

OBJECTIVES:
- To improve usage and understanding of adjectives.
- To improve usage and understanding of synonyms.
- To improve vocabulary skills.
- To improve creative thinking.
- To improve strategies for success.
- To improve teamwork and cooperation.

TARGET POPULATION: Grades 2-5

MATERIALS:
- Noun pair list (provided)
- Paper and pencil for each student
- Chalkboard and chalk

PROCEDURE: Divide students into teams of three or four. Designate one member of each team to be recorder and give each recorder paper and a pencil.

On the chalkboard write one pair of nouns from the provided list, leaving a blank line before each word. Instruct teams to work together to choose *one* adjective that could correctly be used to describe *each* of the given nouns. The recorder will write the team's consensus on his paper.

When all teams are ready, ask each to reveal its response. If the answer is an adjective, describes both given nouns, *and no other team has selected that adjective*, the team scores a point. "Used" adjectives may not be reused for any noun pairs during the remainder of the activity. The use of synonyms, however, should be encouraged.

Play continues with other noun pairs for as long as time allows. The team with the highest point total wins.

MODIFICATIONS: Write all "used" adjectives on a piece of chart paper that can be saved as a word bank for future writing assignments.

Noun Pair List

a baby and a party
a baseball and a football
a giraffe and a building
a book and a movie
a flower and hair
bubbles and a balloon
a dog and a bed
a pilot and a plumber
a painting and a rainbow
a pencil and a pretzel
a baby doll and a mouse
greeting cards and posters
a dentist and a teacher
a fork and a paper clip

a belt and a necklace
a rainbow and a butterfly
a drink and the river
a suitcase and a dresser
a skunk and a zebra
the weather and a mirror
a pizza and perfume
a child and a cookie
a mountain and a ladder
gravy and whipped cream
a shoe lace and spaghetti
a song and a TV commercial
a globe and a wheel
a hair dryer and a stove

hair and fur
sugar and sand
a rake and a pan
earrings and gloves
popcorn and pretzels
a car and a gun
a couch and a pillow
a house and a car
a star and the moon
a steak and a potato
a drum and a child
a wheel and a ball
music and poetry
a feather and a leaf

ADJECTIVE DETECTIVE

OBJECTIVES:
To improve usage and understanding of adjectives.
To improve vocabulary skills.
To improve strategies for success.
To improve auditory memory skills.
To improve listening skills.
To improve independent decision making.
To improve analytical thinking.

TARGET POPULATION: Grades 2-5

MATERIALS: Sentence list (provided)
Paper and pencil for each student

PROCEDURE: Divide students into teams. Provide each student with a piece of paper and a pencil. Explain that students will be writing down one, *and only one*, adjective from the sentence that will be read. If teams cannot be divided evenly, it will be necessary to declare someone from each of the "shorted" teams to be the "double respondent". This person can write two adjectives for each sentence. Teammates could take turns being the "double respondent". This ensures that all teams are given an equal number of responses per sentence. Students will be working independently, but scoring points for their teams.

Read a sentence from the provided list three times so that no one must ask for repetition. Explain that team points will be kept, and that points will be earned as follows: If a student writes a word that is actually used as an adjective in the given sentence, *and no more than three students from the class have chosen that same adjective*, each of the students who has written that adjective scores one point for his team. It is possible that all of the points may go to the same team. Explain to students that it is to their advantage to choose an adjective that they think few others will choose. Copying an adjective that someone else has written will decrease the chances of earning points.

When all students are ready with one written adjective, begin checking responses. Reread the sentence with a pause between each word. When the student hears the teacher say the word that he has written, he must immediately raise his hand or be left out of the count. Tally each point as it is earned. Be sure to inform students which words are adjectives in the sentence even if no one has selected a particular adjective. Also explain why incorrect responses are not adjectives in that sentence.

Continue by reading the next sentence three times and following the same procedure. The team with the most points at the end of the session is declared the winner.

Note: In the given sentences articles are included as adjectives. Although they are indeed adjectives, it may be wise to exclude them from the choice of adjectives that students may select. This will stop students from always choosing "a", "an" or "the".

MODIFICATIONS: Deduct a point from a team if one of its members writes a word that is not used as an adjective in the given sentence.

After scoring each sentence read the "boring" sentence that remains after all adjectives are removed. They will sound much like newspaper headlines.

ADJECTIVE DETECTIVE
Sentence List

Many sleeveless yellow shirts are on sale at that new clothing store.
My old blue doll was destroyed by a huge black pickup truck.
Several lonely old ladies met for a long lunch at the new Chinese restaurant.
Our crazy uncle decided to wear blue striped pants with a red dotted shirt.
That green wooden chair had three loose squeaky legs.
Mom ordered hot black coffee, a small fish sandwich and extra tartar sauce.
I saw the young princess in a beautiful white gown and a sparkling diamond tiara.
Her cousin told an unbelievable story about a wild rock concert and fifteen problem kids.
As we walked down the lonely mountain trail we noticed the colorful oak leaves.
This cheap plastic watch fell from my skinny wrist and broke on the hard concrete floor.
Both girls needed a large cardboard box, some red construction paper and a sharp knife.
Under the kitchen table I found a shiny new penny and some other coins for my piggy bank.
The tasty rice casserole was prepared by a fantastic Italian chef for a special occasion.
Those difficult math problems were checked by our substitute teacher and some volunteer helpers.
My bratty brother took the unopened birthday presents and hid them in a dark closet in dad's room.
This precious little puppy was playing with a soft rubber toy in the crunchy white snow.
A heavy wooden beam fell on Bob's left foot during our last soccer match.
Many small children were playing in the cool country stream on that hot day.
His sister's best art project won the grand prize at our county fair.
The music teacher asked her top students to choose a lengthy serious novel from the school library.

IT'S ALL THE SAME

OBJECTIVES: To improve usage and understanding of adjectives.
To improve usage and understanding of synonyms.
To improve vocabulary skills.

TARGET POPULATION: Grades 2-5

MATERIALS: Sentence list (provided)
Chalkboard and chalk

PROCEDURE: Divide the class into teams. Read one sentence from the provided sentence list to the entire class. The first person from team 1 will respond by attempting to repeat the sentence *with one modification.* After determining for himself the adjective in the sentence, the student must change that adjective to another adjective with the same or very similar meaning. For example, if the original sentence is "We had a marvelous day at the beach", the student's response may be "We had a wonderful day at the beach". If the student correctly determined the adjective to be replaced from the original sentence, he earns one point for his team. If his replacement adjective was a synonym of the originally used adjective, he scores an extra point. If no points are scored by this player, the first player from team 2 gets a chance to respond to the same sentence. If a point is scored, write the "used" adjective(s) on the chalkboard so that they may not be reused, and then read a new sentence from the list to the next team.

When writing "used" adjectives on the chalkboard, group them in pairs if they are indeed synonyms, or write the synonym pairs on chart paper and post the chart in the classroom as a word bank for creative writing lessons.

Continue playing until everyone has had a turn. It may be necessary to let one person from some of the teams respond again in order to ensure that all teams have had an equal number of chances to earn points. The team with the most points at the end of play is the winner.

MODIFICATIONS: After points are scored for a particular sentence, ask for volunteers to state other adjectives which could have been used as synonyms. Award no points for these answers, but include them on your synonym list as described above.

Award an extra point to any player who on his turn is successfully able to provide two adjective synonyms for a given sentence.

Continue the activity as described above, making sure that two synonyms are given before moving on to the next sentence.

IT'S ALL THE SAME
Sentence List

A little child interrupted me.	(small, tiny...)
We saw a magnificent display of fireworks.	(superb, fantastic...)
There were rats in the unoccupied house.	(empty, vacant...)
The fast rabbit got away from Joey.	(quick, speedy...)
We wish you a merry holiday.	(jolly, happy...)
The whimpering baby could not get to sleep.	(crying, blubbering...)
She used a glittery paint on the wagon.	(shiny, sparkly...)
Dad brought us a darling puppy yesterday.	(cute, adorable...)
Bill gave us a startled look.	(surprised, shocked...)
There was a fading image on my TV.	(disappearing, vanishing...)
Mom was feeling anxious because I wasn't home yet.	(worried, nervous...)
Billy ate the entire pie.	(whole, complete...)
I know the right way to do that.	(correct, intended...)
Amy had a nightmare about a gigantic monster.	(huge, enormous...)
All the way home we followed a disabled vehicle.	(broken, non-working...)
I like to fly kites on a gusty day.	(windy, breezy...)
My parents were grateful that you visited.	(thankful, appreciative...)
We heard a groaning man inside the room.	(moaning, wailing...)
The princess wore a beautiful gown to the ball.	(lovely, spectacular...)
The movie was very uninteresting.	(boring, dull...)
Dad complained about the earsplitting music.	(loud, noisy...)
Yesterday was just a lousy day.	(miserable, awful...)
After walking ten miles, my dog was fatigued.	(tired, exhausted...)
The teacher read us a story about a wicked witch.	(evil, nasty...)
Santa Claus looks plump.	(fat, chubby...)
Tyson is a goofy boy.	(silly, ridiculous...)
The ailing tiger would not even eat.	(ill, sick...)

DESCRIBE IT TO THE LETTER

OBJECTIVES: To improve usage and understanding of adjectives.
To improve vocabulary skills.
To improve strategies for success.
To improve teamwork and cooperation.

TARGET POPULATION: Grades 1-5

MATERIALS: Pencil and paper for each team

PROCEDURE: Divide the class into teams and provide each team with a piece of paper and a pencil. Choose someone from each team to be recorder. Instruct each recorder to vertically spell a given noun down the left edge of his paper. Each recorder will write the same noun. For example:

D
O
G

It is then the responsibility of each team to think of one adjective that begins with each letter of the given noun. Each adjective selected and recorded by teams must also be an adjective that could legitimately be used to describe the written noun. Recorders will write their teams' selections horizontally on their papers, using the letters from the written noun as the first letter of their chosen adjectives. Instruct teams to raise their hands when they have recorded one adjective for each letter of the noun. For example:

Dirty
Old
Graceful

When all teams are ready or when a specified amount of time has elapsed, announce that no more recording may be done. Ask each recorder to announce the adjective that his team has selected for the first letter of the noun. Any team that selects a legitimate adjective earns one point *if no other team has selected the same adjective.* Continue by asking for adjectives which begin with the second letter of the noun, etc. When all adjectives for the given noun have been revealed and all scores have been tallied, choose a new noun for recorders to write vertically down the page.

To assure that teams will not try to repeat adjectives from the first round, try to avoid using new nouns which contain the same letters as the first. For example: "fan", "nest", "lips", or "cub" could be used as the next noun. Longer nouns could include: "sandwich", "monster", family", "music", "spring", "festival", "quarterback", "snowflake", and "children".

Suggestion: Before beginning the activity with younger students it may be beneficial to brainstorm with the class a list of adjectives which begin with each of the vowels.

MODIFICATIONS:

ADJECTIVE CHALLENGE

OBJECTIVES:
To improve usage and understanding of adjectives.
To improve usage and understanding of nouns.
To improve teamwork and cooperation.
To improve vocabulary skills.
To improve strategies for success.
To improve creative thinking.

TARGET POPULATION: Grades 2-5

MATERIALS: Adjective list (provided)
Chalkboard and chalk

PROCEDURE: Divide the class into four teams. Appoint one person from each team to be the recorder.

Write on the chalkboard a group of three adjectives from the provided list. Define any adjectives which are unfamiliar to students. Teammates confer and decide on <u>one</u> noun that can accurately be described by the three given adjectives. Each team's recorder goes to the chalkboard when she is ready to respond. When all four teams are ready, the recorders from each team simultaneously write their noun on the chalkboard and then return to their seats. Check each response. If a written noun does not fit the category, explain why, and award no points to that team. If a team's selected noun is an appropriate one, and no other team has chosen the same word, the team gets four points. If two teams have chosen the same appropriate noun, each earns three points. If three teams match, two points are awarded. If all four teams have identical correct answers, each receives one point. Tally the score for each team. Remind students that choosing an unusual noun, if correct, will earn more points.

Begin round two by selecting a new recorder for each team. Write a new set of three adjectives on the chalkboard and follow the same procedure. Play continues at least until everyone has had the chance to be recorder. The team with the most points at the end of play is declared the winner.

MODIFICATIONS: After each round ask for a volunteer to use the three adjectives and one of the nouns in a grammatically correct sentence. Bonus points may be awarded for this.

Ask for suggestions for other adjectives that could further describe the nouns chosen by each team.

Adjective List

sleek, fast, beautiful
comfortable, strong, blue
pointy, long, wooden
fluffy, soft, graceful
crooked, sturdy, brown
delicious, nutritious, chewy
electric, entertaining, expensive
American, colorful, familiar

smooth, hard, brown
hairy, nasty, scary
minty, sticky, sweet
interesting, unique, magical
furry, agile, funny
powerful, respected, old
fragile, shiny, new
jagged, rough, dirty

tall, wide, smelly
cold, wet, white
fragrant, red, natural
plaid, soft, old
flexible, talented, young
lacey, pink, romantic
moist, alive, green
crowded, hot, noisy

PICTURE THIS

OBJECTIVES: To improve usage and understanding of adjectives.
To improve vocabulary skills.
To improve strategies for success.
To improve teamwork and cooperation.
To improve association skills.

TARGET POPULATION: Grades 2-5

MATERIALS: Noun list (provided)
Pencils and paper for each team
Chalkboard and chalk

PROCEDURE: Divide the class into teams, and provide each team with paper and a pencil. Designate one player from each team to be the recorder.

Choose a noun from the provided list and tell it to the class. Each team will then compile a list of adjectives which appropriately describes that noun. The recorder writes the list suggested by her teammates. After a few minutes call on the recorder from Team 1 to read two adjectives from her list. Write the adjectives on the board under "Team 1". Then call on the next recorder to read two adjectives from her list. Write them on the board under "Team 2". Since points will be awarded only for *unduplicated* adjectives, each recorder should choose carefully which words she wants written on the board.

Finish writing two adjectives from each team on the board. Then allow each team to state one more adjective from its list, if it has not been previously used. Teams may "pass" if they have no new responses. In this way each team will have an opportunity to earn three points for each noun. Some adjectives may require an explanation before determining if they are appropriate.

Round two begins with a new noun from the list and possibly a new recorder. Continue as time permits. The team with the most words on the board at the end of play is the winner.

MODIFICATIONS: Rounds could be played as above, but in reverse. Announce an adjective, and teams must select a noun which could be described by that adjective.

Noun List

eagle	classmate	guitar	airplane	hair	telephone	flowers
ocean	snake	school	bear	moon	farm	costume
parade	perfume	fire engine	sky	music	zoo	beach
Paris	mountains	army	playground	king	wagon	sweater
tent	witch	salesman	diamond	limosine	quilt	necktie

Adjective List (for modified directions)

slimy	proud	slippery	flat	crunchy	round	funny
hairy	fragile	spoiled	broken	prickly	bald	scary
exciting	loose	leftover	smashed	obnoxious	honest	rusted
jealous	helpful	spooky	young	wild	fatal	deep
wounded	dreadful	gross	fragrant	long	early	plastic

COMPARE THESE

OBJECTIVES: To improve usage and understanding of adjectives.
To improve usage and understanding of comparatives.
To improve vocabulary skills.
To improve strategies for success.

TARGET POPULATION: Grades 2-5

MATERIALS: Noun word pair list (provided)
Pencil and paper for each student
Chalkboard and chalk

PROCEDURE: Divide students into teams. Provide each team with a pencil and piece of paper. Teammates will be able to confer before the designated recorder writes an answer.

Tell students that they will be making comparisons between the nouns that will be written on the chalkboard. To make these comparisons, students must use one of the following forms: adjective + "er", as in "higher"; "more" + adjective, as in "more fun"; or "less" + adjective, as in "less expensive". Give several examples until students understand the task.

Write three pairs of words on the chalkboard and instruct teams to write one comparison for each word pair. Inform them that they are not to reverse the order of words within the pairs. For example, if the word pair is "horses - mice", students must be able to say "Horses are _______ than mice." An acceptable answer would be "Horses are stronger than mice". Students may not rearrange the pair so that "mice" preceeds "horses". Inform each team that one point will be given for a correct, sensible answer, *if no other team has chosen the same answer*. Also, once an answer has been used, it may not be reused throughout the activity.

When all teams are ready with their three word-pair comparisons, ask each recorder to reveal his team's answer for the first pair. Award points and then check answers for the next pair of words.

When all answers have been revealed and scored, write three new word pairs on the board. Continue the activity as long as time permits. The team with the most points at the end of play is declared the winner.

MODIFICATIONS:

Noun Word-Pair List

typewriters/computers	gravel/blacktop	oranges/bananas	snow/rain
bubbles/balloons	crackers/cookies	tents/trailers	books/movies
tacos/hamburgers	flowers/grass	airplanes/birds	babies/adults
celery/radishes	songs/poems	mountains/hills	tires/steering wheels
mustard/mayonnaise	glass/wood	eagles/robins	hair/straw
whipped cream/butter	winter/summer	rivers/oceans	circles/squares
New York City/your town	snakes/worms	sweaters/socks	diamonds/rocks
photographs/drawings	schools/churches	guitars/harmonicas	sun/moon
fire engines/motorcycles	beaches/forests	wagons/buses	neckties/belts
CDs/cassette tapes	sirens/school bells	slippers/boots	refrigerators/stoves

A-B-C ADJECTIVES

OBJECTIVES: To improve usage and understanding of adjectives. To improve creative thinking.

TARGET POPULATION: Grades 2-5

MATERIALS: Sentence list (provided)
Chalkboard and chalk

PROCEDURE: Read aloud one sentence from the provided list or, if desired, write it on the chalkboard. Choose any student to begin. Ask her to complete the given sentence with an adjective that begins with the letter "A". She must state the entire sentence and include an adjective that begins with "A". The next student completes the same sentence, choosing an adjective that begins with the letter "B". Continue calling on students, advancing one letter of the alphabet each time. Round one is over when all 26 letters have been completed. To expedite the game, however, the letters "Q", "X", and /or "Z" may be omitted.

If a student cannot think of an adjective that begins with the letter she must use, ask for volunteers to supply an answer. Then allow the same student to try again with the next letter.

Round two, if time allows, begins with a new sentence from the list.

The adjectives chosen as descriptors should make sense. For example, a barn can be "lively" if the animals are noisy, but it will never be "lazy". Determining the appropriateness of an adjective may sometimes require further explanation from the student who suggested it. Accept adjectives that the students can justify or defend.

MODIFICATIONS: The list of adjectives can be written on the board as the activity continues. When all students have responded, or when "Z" is completed, turn the class's attention to the list on the chalkboard. Challenge students to think of one new noun that each of the written adjectives could describe.

The activity can be played as a memory game by requiring each student to repeat in order all adjectives that previous students have stated, and then to add a new adjective that begins with the next letter of the alphabet. For example, "My grandfather's beard is awful, brown, clean and darling." This can quickly become very challenging.

Change the sentence after ten or twelve students have responded.

Sentence List

My grandfather's beard is ________.
The video game was ________.
Uncle Floyd's closet was ________.
Dinosaurs were ______.
Sometimes I feel ________.
She read us a story that was ________.
Her hair is ________.
The barnyard was ________.
Her dogs looked ________.
The marching band sounded ________.
Our summer vacation was ________.
Her bridal dress was ________.
The kids on the playground are ________.
That party was ________.
Lately the weather has been ________.
Aren't flowers ________?

I SPY AN ADVERB

OBJECTIVES: To improve usage and understanding of adverbs.
To improve independent decision making.
To improve listening skills.
To improve analytical thinking.

TARGET POPULATION: Grades 2-5

MATERIALS: Sentence list (provided)
Smiley face and sad face cards-
copy for each student from appendix

PROCEDURE: Copy the smiley face cards and sad face cards from the appendix and give one to each student. Instruct the class that they will use the cards to indicate whether an adverb is present in a sentence which will be read to them.

Choose a sentence from the sentence list and read it aloud twice. If a student determines that there is at least one adverb in that sentence, he will prepare to hold up his smiley face card. If he thinks there are no adverbs, he will prepare to hold up his sad face card. Students do not raise the card of their choice until instructed to do so. They should avoid letting other students know which card they have chosen. This can be accomplished by placing the chosen card on top of the unselected one, and then holding both cards together against the chest. When all cards are against their chests, everyone is ready to respond. Say "Raise your cards." All students simultaneously do so with no one being permitted to alter his choice after viewing the selections of others.

By viewing the raised card of each student it is easy to determine who is having difficulty understanding adverbs. State the adverb in the sentence if there is one.

Continue by reading the next sentence and following the same procedure.

MODIFICATIONS: This activity may also be played as a game if the class is divided into teams. Team points can be earned by individual members responding correctly, or by the "spokesperson" of the group who gives the general consensus of the group after discussion. If individual team members are earning points for their teams, be certain that all teams have equal numbers of players.

Sentence List

We were tired, but we kept walking *slowly*.
My brother's team won the baseball game.
Did anyone know that Wyatt went *there*?
My chest pains have stopped *completely*.
Some kids would like to be actors or actresses.
The man who designed the bridge is my father.
Tomorrow is my birthday.
The thief *carelessly* left a set of fingerprints.
We can see that movie *next*.
I love my radical new school clothes.
The airlines should offer us a special deal.
Bring the children and their parents *here*.
The judge *thoroughly* reviewed the case.
Mrs. Wells picked up her supplies *Friday*.
The pirate's treasure was *never* found.
They will go *later* to get the tickets.
The company can produce them *cheaply*.
I gave my sister a bite of my candy bar.
Mom said I should *always* brush my teeth.
Did you hear the new church bell?

(Adverbs are underlined.)

CAN YOU VERB ADVERBLY?

OBJECTIVES: To improve usage and understanding of adverbs.
To improve usage and understanding of verbs.
To improve creative thinking.
To improve vocabulary skills.
To communicate effectively.
To increase the ability to construct grammatically correct, logical sentences.

TARGET POPULATION: Grades 2-5

MATERIALS: Verb list (provided)
Adverb list (provided)
Paper and pencil for each student

PROCEDURE: Divide students into teams of equal numbers. Ask each student to write two numbers from 1-50 on his paper. He may write the same number twice if he chooses. The first number that he writes will correspond to a verb from the provided list. The second number will denote an adverb from the adverb list. When everyone has two numbers, inform each student of the two words that he has selected. Instruct students to write their words to eliminate forgetfulness. It does not matter if several students choose the same number from either list as long as both numbers are not the same.

Each student working independently must attempt to produce a logical sentence in which his chosen adverb can be used to modify his chosen verb. The exact form of the verb may be altered for tense or subject/verb agreement. Students should write their sentences so that they will not forget them while waiting to respond. When everyone has finished or a specified amount of time has elapsed, ask each student to state his adverb and verb and to read the sentence that he has written. If a student has successfully created a logical sentence in which his adverb modifies his verb, he earns two points for his team. If the student cannot think of such a sentence, he is still able to earn one point by using both words in a single sentence. For example, if the student's words are "slowly" and "raced", the student can earn a single point by writing a sentence such as, "We walked slowly as the cars raced by."

Take turns calling on students to read their sentences. At times an explanation may be required in order to determine if the student's sentence makes sense. For example, the student may write, "He raced slowly to the finish line." A first reaction might be that the sentence is illogical, but if the student explains that he once entered his pet turtle in a turtle race, and it took a long time to go ten feet, points should be awarded.

If time allows after all have responded, let each student select two new numbers and begin again. Do not allow anyone to pick the same adverb or verb that he has previously chosen.

When play is completed the team with the most points is declared the winner.

MODIFICATIONS: When telling students the two words that they have selected, whisper them or point to them on your list. Do not ask students to reveal their words before stating their sentences. After a sentence is read ask for volunteers to guess the adverb and the verb that were chosen.

Do not allow students to suggest negative statements such as "You can't race slowly".

CAN YOU VERB ADVERBLY?

Verb List

1. eat
2. cry
3. jump
4. wait
5. hit
6. stop
7. sit
8. drive
9. laugh
10. sew
11. play
12. make
13. spell
14. read
15. write
16. sing
17. think
18. try
19. work
20. explain
21. act
22. go
23. tackle
24. swim
25. see
26. watch
27. throw
28. cook
29. bend
30. fly
31. fix
32. dance
33. whistle
34. answer
35. ride
36. build
37. camp
38. tease
39. crawl
40. clean
41. talk
42. spin
43. paint
44. wrap
45. dive
46. blow
47. color
48. draw
49. grow
50. cut

Adverb List

1. neatly
2. logically
3. quietly
4. high
5. elegantly
6. completely
7. happily
8. quickly
9. clearly
10. nervously
11. always
12. expertly
13. sloppily
14. awkwardly
15. selfishly
16. nicely
17. wildly
18. casually
19. alone
20. terribly
21. sweetly
22. loudly
23. carefully
24. well
25. superbly
26. ridiculously
27. gracefully
28. swiftly
29. correctly
30. patiently
31. reluctantly
32. foolishly
33. totally
34. never
35. weirdly
36. skillfully
37. pleasantly
38. strangely
39. slowly
40. early
41. accurately
42. wastefully
43. wonderfully
44. lightly
45. deeply
46. fully
47. effortlessly
48. playfully
49. exactly
50. tearfully

ADVERB BINGO

OBJECTIVES: To improve usage and understanding of adverbs.
To improve auditory memory skills.
To improve listening skills.

TARGET POPULATION: Grades 3-5

MATERIALS: Sentence list (provided)
Adverb Bingo grids (provided)-copy one per student
Pencils and/or crayons

PROCEDURE: Give each student a copy of the Adverb Bingo grid, which includes a list of thirty common adverbs. Tell students to complete their grids by writing a different adverb from the list in each of the sixteen squares. Students may choose whichever adverbs they want and write them in any order. Each bingo card prepared in this manner will be unique.

When each student has completed her bingo card, instruct all students to listen to the sentences that will be read. They must listen for the *TWO* adverbs that will be in each sentence. If a student hears an adverb that is on her bingo card, she is to mark an X in the square where the adverb appears.

Slowly and clearly read the first sentence several times without giving emphasis to the adverbs. Keep track of used adverbs to make it easier to check winning cards.

The first student to mark out (X) four adverbs in a row, either horizontally, vertically, or diagonally, calls out "Bingo". Ask the student who called "Bingo" to name the four adverbs that resulted in her win. Check your list to make sure the win is legitimate.

Have the winner appropriately use each of her adverbs in a sentence to get credit for the "Bingo". Play may continue until three or four other students have also achieved a win.

Play a new game with the same grids, this time having students use crayons as markers. In this way they will be able to differentiate words marked from round one.

MODIFICATIONS: The game can be played in pairs with two students sharing one bingo card. This format will assist students who might be having difficulty functioning independently.

This activity could easily be adapted for use with another part of speech.

Sentence List

She easily performed the flip today.
They work there and do their jobs well.
It's too bad that the roof was badly damaged.
Mrs. Fox calmly told the children to run fast.
Hal really wanted Alex to come home soon.
Grace was very happy to go sailing often.
I ran gracefully and did the jumps perfectly.
Jamie slowly approached the lion who was growling loudly.
Luckily Dad arrived home early.
The dog suddenly ran outside.
Later in the day the two boys ran away.
Everywhere I could see the birds clearly.
The maid folded the linens quite neatly.
That lady kindly sewed the torn skirt quickly.
He was soaked rather thoroughly.

(Adverbs are underlined.)

ADVERB BINGO GRID

30 Common Adverbs

easily	perfectly	often	rather	there
neatly	later	slowly	thoroughly	luckily
fast	clearly	very	suddenly	badly
calmly	quite	today	really	gracefully
kindly	too	soon	early	well
outside	quickly	away	everywhere	loudly

ADJECTIVE, ADVERB, NEITHER

OBJECTIVES: To improve usage and understanding of adjectives.
To improve usage and understanding of adverbs.
To improve independent decision making.
To improve listening skills.
To improve auditory memory skills.

TARGET POPULATION: Grades 2-5

MATERIALS: Sentence list (provided)
#1, #2 and #3 cards-copy one per student from appendix
Chalkboard and chalk

PROCEDURE: Give each student a #1 card, a #2 card and a #3 card. On the chalkboard write the following answer key for the number cards:

#1=ADJECTIVE #2=ADVERB #3=NEITHER AN ADJECTIVE NOR AN ADVERB

Instruct students that holding up a #1 card indicates that they have chosen "adjective" as an answer, #2 means "adverb", etc. Make sure that all students understand this correspondence by asking them to hold up the card that means "adjective"... When students understand the correspondence, begin.

Tell the class the target word for the first sentence chosen from the provided list, and then read the sentence. Instruct students that they are to determine if the target word was used as an adjective, an adverb or neither in the given sentence. For example, if the target word is "quiet", and the sentence is "I like to listen to quiet music", students who understand the instructions and the concepts will prepare to hold up their #1 cards. Each student selects the # card of his choice and holds it against his chest to prevent others from viewing it. The # cards which he has not selected should be turned face down on his desk.

When all students are ready, say "Raise your cards", and all students should do so simultaneously. No student is permitted to change his selection at this point. It is now easy to identify those students who are having difficulty understanding adjectives and/or adverbs.

Continue the activity with another target word and sentence.

MODIFICATIONS: This activity may be played as a game if the class is divided into teams. Team points can be earned by individual members responding correctly, or by the spokesperson of the group being correct when reporting the consensus of the group. If individual players are earning points for their teams, be certain that all teams have an equal number of players.

ADJECTIVE, ADVERB, NEITHER
Sentence List

strong	The foundation of the house was very strong.	(adj)
neatly	Her long hair was neatly braided.	(adv)
singing	The song he was singing was a folk tune.	(neither)
old	The burlap lampshade was old and torn.	(adj)
calico	Which of the calico kittens do you want?	(adj)
very	Digging in the garden always gets my hands very dirty.	(adv)
road	The hornet's nest was high above the road.	(neither)
quickly	They left the house and drove quickly to the hospital.	(adv)
antique	She repaired the antique vase carefully.	(adj)
again	The blues album was playing again.	(adv)
extra	We ordered a large pizza with extra pepperoni.	(adj)
raging	We went out into the raging snowstorm.	(adj)
long-stemmed	Mr. Taylor gave Dorie some gorgeous long-stemmed roses.	(adj)
skateboards	Phil and I both have radical skateboards.	(neither)
viciously	The dog growled viciously at the stranger.	(adv)
mean	Harold played a mean trick on his sister.	(adj)
cards	The teacher gave out the report cards.	(neither)
immediately	The principal told us to get to class immediately.	(adv)
nearly	A car nearly hit that tree last night.	(adv)
later	Let's go to the movies later.	(adv)
yesterday	Sam bought a new bicycle yesterday.	(adv)
only	You're the only one who doesn't like ice cream.	(adj)
stained	Her shirt was ripped and stained.	(adj)
dangerous	Skiing can be a dangerous sport.	(adj)
easily	I'm sure Sean can do that easily.	(adv)
threw	He threw the ball to the third baseman.	(neither)
slimy	The slimy bug crawled lazily along his arm.	(adj)
shiny	He just waxed his car so it's really shiny.	(adj)
street	Their new house is right on your street.	(neither)
pointy	The witches' hats were black and pointy.	(adj)
carefully	The soldier's uniform had been carefully pressed.	(adv)
shrill	The train's whistle was shrill and loud.	(adj)
especially	I especially enjoyed the second song they performed.	(adv)
gently	She tickled me gently with the fluffy feather.	(adv)
scared	The donkey's ridiculous braying scared the baby.	(neither)

ADVERB CHARADES

OBJECTIVES: To improve usage and understanding of adverbs.
To improve vocabulary skills.
To improve creative thinking.

TARGET POPULATION: Grades 3-5

MATERIALS: Adverb list (provided)
Sentence list (provided)
Chalkboard and chalk

PROCEDURE: Write one of the sentences from the provided list on the board. Select one student to come forward, and whisper to her an adverb from the provided list. Be careful to select an adverb that will meaningfully fit into the sentence on the board. The student without talking or using his voice must then act out the adverb as it applies to that sentence. Allow students to guess the adverb that she is trying to convey. When someone correctly guesses the adverb, have that student read the sentence on the board, including the pantomimed adverb. The student who guessed correctly then comes forward and is given a new adverb to act out.

Change sentences on the board after every three or four turns. If a student who has already pantomimed guesses another adverb correctly before all other students have done so, allow that student to choose a classmate who has not yet had a turn.

The game is over when everyone has pantomimed or when time expires.

MODIFICATIONS: The class can be divided into two teams. Allow only the teammates of the pantomiming student to guess the adverb. If the team is successful within a given amount of time, award one point.

A selection of adverbs may be written on the board before any student performs. Classmates must choose from these adverbs when guessing. Limit the number of guesses.

Sentence List

The old man walked ________.
The clown drove ________.
The baby ate ________.
The frog jumped ________.
Our class painted ________.
The girl laughed ________.
Her kite flew ________.

The dog chewed ________.
The bird flew ________.
My uncle works ________.
The couple danced ________.
The horse ran ________.
The teacher sang ________.
His feet moved ________.

Adverb List

loudly	weirdly	painfully	slowly	quickly	shyly	high
calmly	cautiously	easily	smoothly	barely	quietly	boldly
passionately	thoughtfully	importantly	greedily	carefully	comfortably	erratically
confidently	dramatically	silently	proudly	fast	suddenly	awkwardly
continuously	gracefully	neatly	wildly	gently	beautifully	sloppily

HOW'D THEY DO THAT?

OBJECTIVES: To improve usage and understanding of adverbs.
To improve usage and understanding of verbs.
To improve strategies for success.
To improve creative thinking.
To improve vocabulary skills.

TARGET POPULATION: Grades 2-5

MATERIALS: Paper and pencil for each team

PROCEDURE: Divide the class into teams and provide each with a piece of paper and a pencil. Choose someone from each team to be recorder. Instruct each recorder to vertically write the same given verb down the left edge of his paper. For example:

R
U
N

It is then the responsibility of each team to think of one adverb that begins with each letter of the given verb. Each adverb selected and recorded by teams must also be an adverb that could legitimately be used to modify the verb. Recorders will write their teams' selections horizontally on their papers, using the letters from the written verb as the first letter of their chosen adverbs. Instruct teams to notify you when they have recorded one adverb for each letter of the verb. For example:

Ridiculously
Uniquely
Noisily

When all teams are ready or when a specified amount of time has elapsed, allow no more writing. Ask all recorders to announce the adverb that their teams have selected for the first letter of the verb. Any team that selects a legitimate adverb earns one point if, and only if, *no other team has selected that same adverb.* Continue by asking for adverbs which begin with the second letter of the verb, etc. When all adverbs for the given verb have been revealed and all scores have been tallied, have recorders turn their papers over and write another verb vertically down the page.

To assure that teams will not repeat adverbs from the first verb given, choose another verb which does not contain any of the same letters as the first. For example: "bat", dip", "go" or "leap" could be used next. Additional verbs would include "eat", "rest", "hop" and "hug".

Suggestion: Before beginning this activity it may be beneficial to brainstorm with the class a list of adverbs which begin with each of the vowels.

MODIFICATIONS: ✋ ❖ ✍ ♈

MOVABLE ADVERBS

OBJECTIVES: To improve usage and understanding of adverbs.
To improve sentence structure.
To improve vocabulary skills.
To communicate effectively.
To increase the ability to construct grammatically correct, logical sentences.

TARGET POPULATION: Grades 3-5

MATERIALS: Sentence list (provided)
Chalkboard and chalk
Adverb list-see "Parts of Speech Sample List" in appendix

PROCEDURE: Choose a sentence from the provided list and write it on the chalkboard leaving a space between each word. Then ask for a volunteer to state one adverb that could be appropriately used in the sentence. Ask the same student to repeat the sentence which will now include his adverb. If the adverb is used appropriately, place an asterisk (*) on the chalkboard to indicate the placement of the adverb in the sentence. For example, if the sentence is "The maid cleaned the house", and a student selects "reluctantly" as his adverb, ask him to state his new sentence. If he states "The maid reluctantly cleaned the house", place an asterisk between the words "maid" and "cleaned" on the chalkboard. Then ask another volunteer to use the same adverb, but to place it elsewhere in the sentence. Again on the chalkboard place an asterisk to indicate the adverb's placement. When finished, the sentence on the board may look as follows:

* The maid * cleaned the house * .

Then ask for another adverb which could replace "reluctantly" and see if the new adverb could also be inserted into the same spaces. If necessary, refer to the list in the appendix for adverb suggestions.

Point out that prepositional phrases are not divided to insert an adverb, but that entire prepositional phrases can be used as adverbs, such as "in the morning".

Choose a new sentence to write on the board, and repeat the above process.

It may be beneficial to keep a list of "used" adverbs on the board or on chart paper so that students will not repeat. This chart could then be used as a word bank for creative writing lessons.

MODIFICATIONS:

Sentence List

I ran with my dog.
She ate her spaghetti.
Bill read the newspaper.
The music played.
Her parents waited for the news.
The car went through the intersection.
The students moved out of the building.
Someone answered the telephone.
Jeff finished his homework.
The maid cleaned the house.
He returned my money.
The dog attacked my dad.
Mom cooked dinner.
They bought their first home.
She smiled for the photographer.
Tina went to the birthday party.
The robber left the crime scene.
The doctor looked at the x-rays.
David slept in his tent.
He laughed at the joke.

HUNTING FOR PREPOSITIONS

OBJECTIVES: To improve usage and understanding of prepositions.
To improve vocabulary skills.
To improve creative thinking.
To improve association skills.

TARGET POPULATION: Grades 2-5

MATERIALS: Preposition list (provided)

PROCEDURE: Choose a preposition and use it in a sentence which relates to something in the classroom. For example, "The chart is UNDER the clock." Ask students for additional examples of sentences related to the classsroom, using the same preposition. Encourage students to state at least ten sentences for the given preposition before selecting a new one.

Give one example for each new preposition to illustrate its proper usage. If possible, elicit ten appropriate sentences for each.

MODIFICATIONS: In upper grades allow students to actually (and gently) manipulate their classmates into positions which can be used to illustrate the chosen preposition.

To make the activity more challenging, choose two prepositions to be used in the same sentence. For example, "The chart is UNDER the clock and BESIDE the lockers.

Allow students to choose two or more prepositions and draw a picture which illustrates a sentence that they have written on the paper.

Name an object or person in the classroom. Challenge students to describe the object's (or person's) location using as many prepositions as are appropriate.

❄ ✍ ♈ ⌘

Preposition List

before	over	across	behind	at
near	through	above	below	against
between	on	among	beyond	in
under	underneath	by	off	with

PREPOSITION DETECTIVE

OBJECTIVES: To improve usage and understanding of prepositions.
To improve vocabulary skills.
To improve strategies for success.
To improve auditory memory skills.
To improve listening skills.
To improve independent decision making.
To improve analytical thinking.

TARGET POPULATION: Grades 2-5

MATERIALS: Sentence list (provided)
Paper and pencil for each student

PROCEDURE: Divide students into teams. Provide each student with a piece of paper and a pencil. Explain that students will be writing down one, *and only one*, preposition from the sentence that will be read. If teams cannot be divided evenly, it will be necessary to declare someone from each of the "shorted" teams to be the "double respondent". This person can write two prepositions for each sentence, or teammates can take turns being the "double respondent". This ensures that all teams are given an equal number of responses per sentence. Students will be working independently, but scoring points for their teams.

Read a sentence from the provided list three times so that no one must ask for repetition. Explain that team points will be kept, and that points will be earned as follows: If a student writes a word that is actually used as a preposition in the given sentence, and no more than three students from the class have chosen that same preposition, each of the students who has written that preposition scores one point for his team. It is possible that all of the points may go to the same team. Explain to students that it is to their advantage to choose a preposition that they think few others will choose. Copying a preposition that someone else has written will decrease the chances of scoring points.

After reading the sentence three times, all students should be ready with one written preposition. Begin checking responses by rereading the sentence with a pause after each word. When the student hears the word that he has written, he must immediately raise his hand or be left out of the count. Tally each point as it is earned. Be sure to inform students which words are prepositions in the sentence even if some were not selected as responses. Also explain why incorrect responses are not prepositions in that sentence.

Continue by reading the next sentence three times and following the same procedure. The team with the most points at the end of the session is declared the winner.

MODIFICATIONS: Deduct a point from a team if one of its members writes a word that is not used as a preposition in the given sentence.

Students working in teams or individually try to identify all prepositions in a sentence.

PREPOSITION DETECTIVE
Sentence List

The boy with his dog sat on your porch for two hours.
Go to the top of the steps and put this in the basket on the right.
Look under the rug in the corner of your bedroom.
We will walk down this street and toward the church that is on the corner of Elm Street.
All of the students from the high school have gone on a field trip to Disneyworld.
Around the corner from the library is a wall with one hundred names on it.
The racers ran up the hill, through the trees, across the meadow and down the other side.
I hope I sit behind you in math class and beside you during art.
The smell of the doughnuts from the bakery travelled out the door and through the town.
The picture of the baby fell off the wall and landed on the television.
He rubbed the old pages of the book between his fingers and crumbled them onto the floor.
A friend of my mother came to the party with food for everyone.
One of the old clocks at our house is on the floor behind the couch.
A woman standing near me in line at the grocery store had a sack of potatoes.
Over the river and through the woods to Grandmother's house we go.
From the bottom of my heart I want everything for you that you deserve.
She cut all of the sandwiches on the table into small pieces for the toddlers.
Reading the words on that poster is difficult for me without my glasses.
She swept a small amount of dirt under the carpet in the living room.
The road to my house winds around the countryside toward the best part of the beach.
A man with a scar on his face came down the hall, through the gym, and into our classroom.
Under the table is a piece of paper with several words written in Spanish.
Elaine drew a sketch of a girl with a bow in her hair and a belt around her waist.
At summer camp we ran up the trail, down the hill, over the courtyard and toward the school.
After lunch the teacher read a story to us about a boy in high school.
During the day the ducks like swimming along the shore near the mouth of the river.
Dad brought home a stack of movies about horses for us.
Before Christmas I will take a trip from Maine to Ohio on a passenger train.
The boy with red hair stood against the wall and blew bubbles between our legs.
Outside our window was a yellow bird with red wings, and a few green feathers under his beak.
The kids walked along the fence, around the field and beyond the barn.
I sit near Jim who is in front of Andy and behind Tina.
Don't go to the store without money for a carton of eggs.
Run into the cabin and get the lantern that is under the table beside the bag of groceries.
At my house beneath the Christmas tree is a box of gifts for Mom and Dad.
When the climbers got to the top of the hill, they put a flag from their country near the peak.
Once upon a time, even before dinosaurs, the earth was covered with masses of trees.
The kangaroo hopped around the cage and jumped on the food that Ted put by the door.

(Underlined words are prepositions.)

PREPOSITION BINGO

OBJECTIVES: To improve usage and understanding of prepositions.
To improve listening skills.
To improve auditory memory skills.

TARGET POPULATION: Grades 3-5

MATERIALS: Sentence list (provided)
Pencils for each student
Bingo grids-copy one per student

PROCEDURE: Give each student a copy of the Preposition Bingo grid, which includes a list of thirty common prepositions. Tell students to complete their grids by writing one prepostion from the list in each of the sixteen squares. They may choose whichever prepositions they want and write them in any order. Each bingo card prepared in this manner will be unique.

When students have completed their bingo cards, instruct them to listen to the sentence that will be read. They must listen for the two prepositions that will be in the sentence. If either or both of the prepositions are on a student's bingo card, she is to mark an X in the square where the preposition appears. Slowly repeat the sentence two or three times without giving emphasis to the prepositions. Keep track of the prepositions that have been used to make the bingo cards easier to check.

The game proceeds as above with one sentence at a time. The first student to mark (X) four prepositions in a row (vertically, horizontally or diagonally) calls "Bingo". Have that student name the four prepositions that she marked to earn the win. Check to make sure that those prepositions were indeed used in the given sentences.

Have the student use each of her prepositions in a correct sentence to get credit for the win. Play may continue until three or four other students have achieved "Bingo".

MODIFICATIONS: The game could be played in pairs with two students sharing bingo cards. This will help students who might be having difficulty functioning independently.

Sentence List

The play at the old theater lasted about one hour.	(at, about)
Across the field stood a large horse and her colt behind her.	(across, behind)
The plane with the red stripes flew above the clouds.	(with, above)
I was under the trees when the ladder fell against the house.	(under, against)
There was one red leaf among all the green ones on the maple tree.	(among, on)
We'll go to the library before lunch.	(to, before)
Shannon walked toward the pool which was just beyond the ballfield.	(toward, beyond)
Between the garage and the shed was a row of roses.	(between, of)
Janie walked into the gym during sixth period.	(into, during)
She ate all the fruit from the grocery store except the strawberries.	(from, except)
The dog in that car looks like a friendly animal.	(in, like)
Near the lake is a good spot for a picnic.	(near, for)
The button fell off the table by the refrigerator.	(off, by)
Sam and Katie raced their bikes through the long tunnel and out the other side.	(through, out)
As our helicopter flew over the ocean we could see fish just below the surface.	(over, below)

PREPOSITION BINGO GRID

Preposition List

about
across
above
against
among
at

before
behind
below
between
beyond
by

during
except
for
from
in
into

like
near
of
on
out
off

over
through
to
toward
under
with

PREPOSITION ADDITION

OBJECTIVES: To improve usage and understanding of prepositions.
To improve sentence structure.
To communicate effectively.
To increase the ability to construct grammatically correct, logical sentences.
To improve creative thinking.

TARGET POPULATION: Grades 3-5

MATERIALS: Sentence list (provided)
Preposition cards-copy from appendix
Paper and pencil for each group
Chalkboard and chalk

PROCEDURE: Divide the class into small groups. Select a sentence from the provided list and write it on the chalkboard or on a sentence strip. Ask one student from each group to draw one card from the facedown pile of shuffled preposition cards (provided). After drawing the card each student returns to his group to decide on an expanded sentence which can be made by adding a prepositional phrase to the sentence on the board. The prepositional phrase must begin with the preposition that was on the card drawn by each group. For example, if the sentence on the board is "The girl brought a book", and . . .

the selected preposition card is:	acceptable sentences could include:
in	The girl in the blue coat brought a book. In June the girl brought a book. The girl brought a book in her satchel.
with	The girl with red hair brought a book. The girl brought a book with pictures. With pride the girl brought a book.

When all groups are ready ask someone from each group to state its sentence. Points can be awarded, if desired, for correct responses. Additional points could be earned by any group that successfully inserts an appropriate prepositional phrase in various locations within one sentence. Point out that there may be some sentences, however, that may not be usable with specific prepositions. In this case, give a point to the team that indicates that its preposition *cannot* be used with the given sentence. If, however, another team can think of an acceptable sentence, award them the point.

After collecting and reshuffling cards, write the next sentence on the board. Select another student from each group to draw one. Repeat the procedure above. Continue as long as time allows. The team with the highest point total is declared the winner.

MODIFICATIONS: ✋ ❖ ✍ ♈ ⌘

Sentence List

Howard ate his dinner.
The police caught the criminal.
Stephen broke his glasses.
Someone took the cassette tape.
My parents love that music.
The zookeeper fed the animals.
The flowers may bloom late.
Dad will buy a new radio.
The story ended suddenly.
Her dog ate the cookies.
The party was over early.
Everything was considered a treasure.
The house was built last year.
No one could hear the speaker.
Wyatt will work tonight.
The building may be torn down.

PREP-POSITIONING

OBJECTIVES: To improve usage and understanding of prepositions.
To improve vocabulary skills.
To improve creative thinking.
To improve analytical thinking.
To communicate effectively.

TARGET POPULATION: Grades 2-5

MATERIALS: Preposition list (provided)
Chalkboard and chalk

PROCEDURE: Name an object or person in the classroom, or select a commonplace occurence, such as recess. Call on one student at a time to describe the location of the named noun relative to something else within the room. The location should include a prepositional phrase.

For example, if a particular child is the designated noun, his location may be described in various ways, such as "between Jim and Amy", "behind Jared", "at the corner", "in the middle row", "on the chair", etc. If an occurence such as recess is the noun to target, it can be described as "after lunch", "on the playground", "during the noon hour", "with Mrs. Coleman", etc.

As each prepositional phrase is correctly used, write it on the chalkboard and underline the preposition. Then give students another target noun to describe or locate. Challenge the class to use a variety of prepositions. Refer to the provided preposition list.

MODIFICATIONS: The activity can be done as a game with the class divided into teams. Each team confers to compile a list of prepositional phrases which locate or describe a target noun. Points are awarded for each correct description that uses a different preposition.

The preposition list could be written on the board to generate a large variety of responses.

Preposition List

about	before	during	like	over
behind	beside	beyond	except	near
across	through	above	below	for
of	to	against	onto	between
at	from	on	toward	under
among	by	in	into	out
off	with	without	beneath	around

PREPOSITION POSITION

OBJECTIVES: To improve usage and understanding of prepositions.
To improve vocabulary skills.
To improve following direction skills.
To improve listening skills.
To improve association skills.

TARGET POPULATION: Grades 1-4

MATERIALS: Shapes/Numbers/Letters page-copy one per student from appendix
Question list (provided)

PROCEDURE: Distribute copies of the shape sheets, or enlarge one copy onto tagboard for display.

Number students where they sit. The first student is #1, the second is #2, the third is #1... until all students are numbered as team #1 or team #2. Begin with the first student and read a question from the provided list. If he responds correctly after hearing the question only once, he earns two points for his team. If he is incorrect, read the question again to the same student, giving one point for a correct answer. The student may then earn an additional point for his team by stating the preposition that was in the question. The question may be read again before requiring the student to state the included preposition. If the student is unable to earn the point for identifying the preposition, ask for volunteers to help out, but award no points.

Repeat the procedure with the next person in the row, a member of team #2. Continue until all students have had the chance to answer at least once. The team with the most points at the end of play is declared the winner.

MODIFICATIONS: For younger students, it may be beneficial to review the names of the given shapes before beginning the activity.

Instead of asking students in lower grades for the preposition, ask "What word told you where to look?"

To accommodate all ranges of abilities ask questions of various levels of difficulty. For example, "What is the sum of the numbers that are inside the diamond and above the square?", or "What vowel is used when you spell the name of the shape that contains the number five?", or "With what letter does the number above the oval start?"

Allow students to make up their own questions related to the shape chart, and to call on other students to give responses.

PREPOSITION POSITION
Question List

What number is under the oval?	(7)
What capital letter is in the rectangle?	(M)
What number is between the heart and the square?	(3)
What capital letter is directly above the star?	(J)
What small shape is within the triangle?	(heart)
What lower case letter is inside the circle?	(a)
What number is on the square?	(6)
What small shape is underneath the diamond?	(square)
What capital letter is beneath the heart?	(E)
What number is closest to the circle?	(2)
What lower case letter is over the triangle?	(e)
What small shape is beside the oval?	(circle)
What small shape is beside the diamond?	(rectangle)
What letter is between the oval and the square?	(z)
What number is within the star?	(5)
What number is closest to the rectangle?	(4)
What small shape is inside the square?	(triangle)
What letter is underneath the circle?	(C)
What number is between the triangle and the diamond?	(8)
What small shape is under the star?	(oval)
What capital letter is over the heart?	(N)
What number is in the diamond?	(9)
What letter is beneath the square?	(K)
What capital letter is beside the triangle?	(Q)
What letter is near the rectangle?	(L)
What number is above the oval?	(10)
What small shape is near the heart?	(star)
What number is closest to the large star?	(17)
What letter is inside the heart?	(v)
What number is between the square and the triangle?	(21)
What letter is on the square?	(x)
What number is between the circle and the square?	(13)
What letter is beneath the diamond?	(Y)
What letter is between the diamond and the star?	(W)
What number is in the oval?	(33)

(Underlined words are prepostions.)

ALL TOGETHER NOW

OBJECTIVES:
- To improve usage and understanding of conjunctions.
- To improve vocabulary skills.
- To improve strategies for success.
- To improve sentence structure.
- To increase the ability to construct grammatically correct, logical sentences.

TARGET POPULATION: Grades 3-5

MATERIALS:
- Sentence pair list (provided)
- Conjunction cards-copy from appendix
- #1 & #2 cards-copy from appendix
- Chalkboard and chalk

PROCEDURE: Divide the class into teams. Give each team a #1 and a #2 card, and one of each of the conjunction cards. Choose a pair of sentences from the provided list and write them on the chalkboard. Label the first sentence #1, and the second #2.

Explain to students that teammates are to determine a way that the two sentences on the board can be connected by using any one of the conjunction cards. The sentences can be combined in either order using any of the conjunction cards, as long as the combined sentence makes sense. If a team decides that sentence #1 comes first, "but" is next, and sentence #2 is last, that team will place its cards in order as such:

#1 "but" #2.

Another team may decide that "although" comes first, then sentence #2, and finally sentence #1. Their cards will be ordered as such:

"although" #2 #1.

Teams should not allow other teams to know ahead of time the answer sequence that they have selected. This can be prevented by placing something over their answers until it is time to respond.

Any team that produces a sentence which makes sense, *in a combination that no other team has chosen*, will earn a point.

Continue with the next pair of sentences from the list. The team with the most points at the end of play is the winner.

MODIFICATIONS: Ask students to tell if each of the given conjunctions can be used with a particular pair of sentences, and if so, to state the location of the conjunction.

Sentence Pair List

My father shook my hand. My mother kissed me.
I was supposed to go to school. Dad told me to stay home.
He might go to the pool. He will probably go to the movies.
She got an "F" on her report card. She was grounded.
He got a bike for his birthday. He wanted to take a ride.
I had pizza for dinner. I really wanted to have hotdogs.
I would like to make that for you. I have no glue.
Very loud thunder started. A mild storm hit the area.
She will try to attend the meeting. She will call if she can't.
The elephants are the heaviest animals here. The giraffes are the tallest.
He wanted to fill the swimming pool. He couldn't turn on the water.
I worked hard. I deserve a raise.
She didn't feel well. She came to school.
I was hungry. I decided to have a snack.
They could watch TV. They could play games.
He went roller skating. He visited his cousins.
I returned from vacation. I was happy to see her.
He wanted to come to my game. He had a headache.
They grow on bushes. They are not edible.

ADDITIONAL THOUGHTS

OBJECTIVES: To improve usage and understanding of conjunctions.
To improve creative thinking.
To improve sentence structure.
To increase the ability to construct grammatically correct, logical sentences.

TARGET POPULATION: Grades 3-5

MATERIALS: Sentence list (provided)
Conjunction cards-copy from appendix
Paper and pencil for each group
Chalkboard and chalk

PROCEDURE: Divide the class into small groups. Select a sentence from the provided list and write it on the chalkboard. Ask one student from each group to draw one card from the face down pile of shuffled conjunction cards (provided). After drawing the card each student returns to his group to write a sentence which uses the conjunction on his card, the sentence on the board, and one additional sentence.

For example, if the sentence on the board is "I got wet", and . . .

the selected conjunction card is:	acceptable sentences would include:
but	I got wet but I didn't care. I got wet but Jeff didn't tell my mom. Bob and Julie stayed dry, but I got wet.
since	Since it was raining, I got wet. I got wet since Ed aimed the hose at me. Since I rode on the waterslide, I got wet.

When all groups are ready, ask someone from each group to read its sentence. Points can be awarded, if desired, for correct responses.

Collect and shuffle the conjunction cards and then write the next sentence on the board. Select another student to draw one. Repeat the above procedure.

MODIFICATIONS: ✋ ❖ ✍ ♈ ⌘

Sentence List

I will get wet.
Amy wants to go home.
You might break your glasses.
The gun will not be loaded.
The carnival will be cancelled.
The house will be finished.
We could go to the movies.
The flowers may die.
Dad will buy a new radio.
Brenda will read you a story.
She might need some money.
John will get sick.
The store won't be open.
We can go tomorrow.
I had to be in the contest.
Grandma will visit us.
The bridge will be closed.
I will work all night.
The building may explode.
The plane will take off.

EXCLAIM THIS!

OBJECTIVES: To improve usage and understanding of interjections.
To improve vocabulary skills.
To improve strategies for success.
To improve creative thinking.
To communicate effectively.

TARGET POPULATION: Grades 3-5

MATERIALS: Sentence list (provided)
Interjection list (provided)
Chalkboard and chalk
Paper and pencil for each student

PROCEDURE: Write the given word bank of interjections on the chalkboard or on a piece of chart paper that can be posted in the classroom for future creative writing assignments. Have all students copy the list onto their own papers.

Divide the class into teams. Students will work independently to score points for their teams.

Read aloud one sentence from the provided sentence list. Each student independently will select from his own list an appropriate interjection that can be meaningfully added to the given sentence. He will identify his choice by circling it on his paper. He may circle *only one* interjection. When all students are ready, ask them to state the interjections that they have chosen. Any student who has chosen an interjection that can be appropriately used in the given sentence earns a point for his team. For example, if the original sentence is, "The mother dog had ten puppies", the four team members from team 1 may answer with the following four responses: "Hurray!", "Wow!", "Heavens!", and "Wow!". As long as each selected interjection can be used appropriately in that particular sentence, team 1 scores four points. If only three of the four selected interjections can be justified, three points are earned, and so on. Some responses may require an explanation from students to determine the validity of a particular interjection.

After all team scores have been recorded, instruct each student to cross his circled interjection from his list. Individual lists will now begin to look different. Students may not again select any interjection which has been crossed off their lists.

Read another sentence from the sentence list. Students again circle one choice from the remaining interjections on their personal lists. Tally points and again instruct students to cross off their "used" interjections. Continue play in this same manner with additional sentences.

Most students will be able to score points for their teams on the initially read sentences, but play will become increasingly difficult, and involve a bit of chance, as the personal interjection lists become smaller. Explain to students that it would be to their advantage, if possible, to save until the end of the game the interjections that they think might fit into a larger variety of sentences, and to select earlier in the game those which have a more limited use. For example, "Oh!" could probably be used in more sentences than "Alas!".

Students <u>must</u> select an interjection for each sentence. This ensures that each student's list shrinks by the same amount. If a student determines that none of his remaining interjections could be justified in a given sentence, he may skip the circling step of the game and simply cross off one interjection. After he has done so, however, he may not claim credit if another student successfully justifies using that same interjection.

EXCLAIM THIS! (continued)

Play continues until all interjections have been used. The team with the most points is declared the winner.

Be certain that all teams have an equal number of players to ensure that every team has the same scoring opportunity. Teams that are shorted a player will need to have one player designated as a "double respondent". This player will have a second list and will select one interjection from each list for each sentence. He may, *but does not have to,* select the same interjection from each list for a given sentence. It may be more fun to allow the "double respondent" to be a different teammate for each sentence. This can be accomplished by passing along the "double respondent's" interjection list.

Students should be encouraged to use appropriate inflection when saying their sentences. This will assist with lessons involving the use of punctuation.

MODIFICATIONS:

Interjection List

Oh!	Uh-oh!	Heavens!	Dear me!	Phooey!
Alas!	Yeah!	Ugh!	Ah!	Aha!
Hurray!	Wow!	Yes!	Ouch!	Hey!

Sentence List

(Select 15 of these sentences for the 15 given interjections.)

I hurt myself.
We're having liver for dinner.
The score of the game was 10-9.
What are we going to do?
Now I know what happened.
We have twelve pages of homework.
The doctor tried to save him, but he died anyway.
The mother dog had ten puppies.
This car costs too much.
That lotion feels great on my sunburn.

We are going to Disneyworld.
I figured out the mystery.
This hot tub feels great.
He asked me to marry him.
My pants are falling down.
I just won the lottery.
Those fireworks were great.
That dress is beautiful.
I know who stole the money.
Your dog almost bit me.

CHOOSE NOW

OBJECTIVES: To improve usage and understanding of conjunctions, interjections, and prepositions.
To improve independent decision making.
To improve vocabulary skills.
To review parts of speech.

TARGET POPULATION: Grades 3-5

MATERIALS: #1, #2, #3 & #4 cards for each team-copy from appendix
Sentence list (provided)
Chalkboard and chalk

PROCEDURE: Divide the class into teams by rows, and give a set of number cards (#1-#4) to the first player on each team. Number the teams and place the team numbers on the "scoreboard" (chalkboard). Also on the chalkboard write the following answer key:

#1=conjunction #2=interjection #3=preposition #4=none of these

Ask the card holders, one person from each team, to stand beside their desks. Instruct them to hold their cards like playing cards in one hand close to their chests so that no one else can see them.

Name a target word from the provided list. Then read aloud the corresponding sentence from the list. The standing students must decide if the target word is being used as a conjunction, preposition, interjection or "none of these". Each of these students then chooses the card that states her choice and lays the other three face down on her desk. Students should not yet reveal their selected card to other students.

When all standing players have made their choices, say "Now". Each of them simultaneously displays the response she has chosen. Score one point for each team whose card holder responded correctly. Each *correct* player then has the opportunity to score an additional point if she can replace the target word with another word that is the same part of speech. For example, "Wow, this soup is too hot!" can be changed to "Yikes, this soup is too hot!". Give each standing player a chance to try for the extra point. If the correct response was "none of these", players may still earn an extra point by selecting any other word in the sentence, and then substituting another word that is the same part of speech. This provides a chance to briefly review other parts of speech.

After scoring the first round of play, the four number cards are passed back to the second person in each row. Each of those students now stands and takes her turn. Play continues in this fashion until all students have had several chances to respond, or as time permits.

The team that has earned the most points at the end of play is the winner.

MODIFICATIONS: ❄ ✋ ❖ ✍ ♈ ⚐
⌘

CHOOSE NOW

Sentence List

although	Her dad goes to church each Sunday although her mother does not.	(conj.)
ouch	Ouch, I just cut my thumb on this sharp edge!	(int.)
around	I walked around the barnyard and the pond.	(prep.)
from	The silvery moon peeked out from the clouds.	(prep.)
but	Sara and Tom walked to the park but they didn't see Felicia.	(conj.)
for	The pot of stew bubbled slowly for hours and hours.	(prep.)
hate	Man, I hate country music!	(none)
wow	Wow, did you see the sunset last night?	(int.)
however	Her flowers were fresh; however, they looked wilted.	(conj.)
or	Did you give her that ring or did she just borrow it?	(conj.)
yet	I studied hard yet I think I failed the exam.	(conj.)
with	Juan's new van is blue with tinted windows.	(prep.)
later	I will do the laundry later today.	(none)
drat	Drat, I missed the hockey playoffs!	(int.)
to	Gracious, what happened to your car?	(prep.)
and	Sheila put the car in reverse and then she parked it.	(conj.)
too	Dave took the telescope out but it was too dark to see.	(none)
on	Six birds landed on the feeder at the same time.	(prep.)
ran	The cats ran away from the frisky pup.	(none)
in	The tall plant in the ceramic bowl needs water.	(prep.)
for	She dug a quarter out of her pocket to pay for the gum.	(prep.)
gosh	Gosh, I am so tired that I can't go out tonight.	(int.)
over	Ken stomped over the pile and sat down.	(prep.)
hallway	Mr. Yost's ruler was lying on the hallway floor.	(none)
but	Suzanne told us a joke but she forgot the punchline!	(conj.)
around	Her favorite horse was running in circles around the barnyard.	(prep.)
humph	Humph! I never got a chance to ride the roller coaster.	(int.)
at	At the mall we saw my Aunt Iris.	(prep.)
oops	Oops, I think I forgot my lunchbox.	(int.)
through	The arrow passed through the bale of hay.	(prep.)
across	Yipes! A mouse just ran across my foot.	(prep.)
and	Her hair is so long and silky.	(conj.)
three	The three houseplants were on the front porch.	(none)
but	Jack took photos with his camera but they didn't turn out well.	(conj.)
zounds	Zounds! That new girl runs fast, and she's smart too.	(int.)
most	Rover ate my hamburger and stole most of my french fries.	(none)
however	Sarah loves picnics; however, she is bothered by the bugs.	(conj.)
above	The American flag flew high above the stadium.	(prep.)
after	The turkeys were squawking loudly after the storm.	(prep.)

WHAT IS IT NOW?

OBJECTIVES: To improve usage and understanding of nouns.
To improve usage and understanding of verbs.
To improve usage and understanding of adjectives.
To improve vocabulary skills.
To improve independent decision making.
To improve analytical thinking.

TARGET POPULATION: Grades 3-5

MATERIALS: Sentence list (provided)
#1, #2, and #3 cards for each student-copy from appendix

PROCEDURE: If possible, divide students into evenly numbered teams. Give each student a #1, a #2, and a #3 card. On the chalkboard write the answer key for the number cards as follows:

#1=NOUN #2=VERB #3=ADJECTIVE

Instruct students that holding up a #1 card indicates that they have chosen "NOUN" as the answer, #2 means VERB, etc. Make sure that this correspondence is understood by all students by asking them to hold up the "VERB" card... When students are ready, begin.

Tell the class the target word for the first sentence, and then read one of the sentences containing that word. Each student individually will decide if the target word in the given sentence is used as a noun, a verb or an adjective, and select the number card that reflects that answer. Students should avoid letting others see their choice by placing the chosen card on top of the other two, and holding all three cards together near the chest.

When everyone is ready say "Raise your cards", and all students simultaneously do so.

Look for the number of correct responses by each team and score one point for each. Inform students of the correct answer and explain if necessary.

Repeat the procedure with a second sentence, using either the same target word or another. Three sentence choices are provided for each target. Continue as time allows.

The team with the most points at the conclusion of the activity is declared the winner.

MODIFICATIONS: ❄ ✋ ⚐ ❖ ♈ ✍
⌘

Sentence List

(tie)
(V) I will tie it in a knot.
(N) The game ended in a tie.
(A) Dad's tie pin was silver and gold.

(box)
(N) Put it in the box.
(V) I am going to box your ears.
(A) Our school is collecting box tops from cereals.

(baby)
(V) Don't baby me any more.
(A) The baby bottle broke in the dishwasher.
(N) Did you call me a baby?

WHAT IS IT NOW? (continued)

(last)	(A) His last name is Monroe. (N) No book is as special as the last. (V) This car will last at least ten years.
(water)	(A) Our water hose has a slow leak. (V) Dad will water the flowers after breakfast. (N) Stay out of the water until after lunch.
(watch)	(A) My watch band needs to be replaced. (V) Will you watch the children for a few minutes? (N) The lieutenant fell asleep during his watch.
(garden)	(V) We garden so that we can have fresh vegetables. (A) I left my garden rake near the pond. (N) Did your garden grow well this year?
(stain)	(N) The stain just would not come out. (V) Mom will stain that chair a walnut color. (A) We can try some stain remover on it.
(punch)	(N) Stacy used pineapple juice in the punch. (A) We bought them a punch bowl for their anniversary. (V) Jack will punch me if I steal his girlfriend.
(date)	(A) I bought a new date book in January. (V) Does Emily date older men? (N) John asked her out on a date.
(fall)	(N) In the fall of each year we go camping. (A) The fall festival was a huge success. (V) Did you fall off the balcony?
(place)	(N) Our neighbors visited a great place on their vacation. (V) Please place this on the kitchen table. (A) She used the leaf as a place marker for her book.
(credit)	(A) Alex stopped at the credit department. (N) Edna deserves all of the credit for the project. (V) The grocery store will credit my account with $10.00.

COMPLETE KINGDOM

OBJECTIVES:
To improve usage and understanding of subjects.
To improve usage and understanding of verbs.
To improve analytical thinking.
To improve listening skills,
To improve auditory memory skills.
To improve teamwork and cooperation.

TARGET POPULATION: Grades 2-5

MATERIALS: Sentence/sentence fragment list (provided)
Job identification cards-copy from appendix
Scotch tape or masking tape
"Gold" (paper clips, bingo chips...)
One "gold" box per kingdom (cup...)

PROCEDURE: Divide students into groups as instructed in the provided class size chart and move groups to areas of the room that will be their "kingdoms". Assign each person in each kingdom a job.

KING (The ruler)---He (male or female) expects everything to be perfect and *complete.* He responds to nothing else.

SUBJECT (The King's royal SUBJECT)---The KING watches over all of his *subjects* (people, places and things), and insists that one of his *subjects* be present for every sentence.

VERB (The most verbal of the kingdom)---The VERB is concerned with the *actions* of the King's *subjects.* He tells the KING what the *subjects* are doing.

HELPING VERB (The VERB's helper)---He *assists* the main VERB if help is needed to complete his actions.

YOU (He understands that he must take orders.)---YOU takes *commands* very well. YOU may be called upon to acccompany the KING when orders are given.

TAILOR (Alters every problem sentence for the KING)---He must stitch *incomplete* sentences together so that they are complete for the KING.

Once jobs have been identified, give each student one of the provided job identification cards. Tape it to his shirt for easy visibility. To begin place five pieces of "gold" in each kingdom's container, and place all containers together for easy access when scoring . Inform kingdoms that you will be reading a sentence or a sentence fragment. Within each kingdom members secretly must decide if the sentence is complete or incomplete, and if incomplete, what is missing. When every kingdom shows that it is ready by having its KING raise his hand, begin checking.

All students should sit on the floor in their kingdoms until the teacher says, "1, 2, 3, stand". Everyone who is going to stand, according to the rules listed later, must do so immediately. After standing, students may not sit back down since they will have had the chance to see who is standing for the other kingdoms. For the same reason, those who did not stand immediately may not change their minds and do so.

To decide who should stand for the kingdom for a particular sentence, follow the given rules. Ignore the rules for jobs that were not assigned in your kingdom due to class size.

COMPLETE KINGDOM (continued)

1. The KING stands if the teacher-read sentence is complete.
2. YOU stands with the KING if the sentence was a command. YOU is truly the subject of the sentence, even though he was not mentioned in it.
3. The SUBJECT stands if the sentence fragment is missing a subject. He does not stand, however, if YOU stands.
4. The VERB stands if the sentence fragment is missing a main verb.
5. The HELPING VERB stands if the sentence fragment is missing a necessary helping verb. If the VERB was present in the sentence, and alone could make a complete sentence, the HELPING VERB does not stand. If the total verb is missing, it is optional for the HELPING VERB to stand.
6. The TAILOR stands if the sentence is incomplete in any way since he is the one who must stitch the complete sentence together. The TAILOR, therefore, will never stand when the KING is standing.

After announcing, "1, 2, 3, stand", go over the sentence/sentence fragment with the class and determine who should be standing for each kingdom. (Before standing, students with two job cards should remove from their shirts the one not needed for that sentence.)

Score each kingdom by putting "gold" in their containers. This prevents students from knowing the running score. For every correct response, a kingdom will earn one piece of gold. Each incorrect response will result in one piece of "gold" being removed from the kingdom's pot. For example, in a given sentence if the subject was missing, only the SUBJECT and the TAILOR should be standing. If, in the given example, one kingdom's SUBJECT, VERB and TAILOR stand, award that kingdom two pieces of "gold" for two correct responses, but then remove one piece of "gold" because VERB should not have stood. If, in the same example, another kingdom's VERB is the only one to stand, remove three pieces of "gold" from that container for three mistakes (SUBJECT, VERB and TAILOR each performed incorrectly).

No kingdom can accumulate a debt. If it has no "gold" to pay, it owes none.

Repeat the procedure by reading another sentence /sentence fragment from the list and awarding or removing pieces of gold from each kingdom's container. When the lesson time expires, count each kingdom's "gold" and declare the richest kingdom the winner.

*** Assign jobs to kingdom members based upon the total number of students in the class.

Class size	Kingdom Make-up	Jobs to Assign in Each Kingdom
28	3 kingdoms of 6, 2 kingdoms of 5	all (one person in kingdoms of 5 is both YOU and TAILOR)
27	2 kingdoms of 6, 3 kingdoms of 5	all (one person in kingdoms of 5 is both YOU and TAILOR)
26	1 kingdom of 6, 4 kingdoms of 5	all (one person in kingdoms of 5 is both YOU and TAILOR)
25	5 kingdoms of 5	all except TAILOR
24	4 kingdoms of 6	all
	or 6 kingdoms of 4	all except YOU and TAILOR
23	3 kingdoms of 6, 1 kingdom of 5	all (one person in kingdom of 5 is both YOU and TAILOR)
22	2 kingdoms of 6, 2 kingdoms of 5	all (one person in kingdoms of 5 is both YOU and TAILOR)
21	1 kingdom of 6, 3 kingdoms of 5	all (one person in kingdoms of 5 is both YOU and TAILOR)
20	4 kingdoms of 5	all except TAILOR
19	3 kingdoms of 5, 1 kingdom of 4	all except TAILOR (one person in kingdom of 4 is both YOU and SUBJ.)
18	3 kingdoms of 6	all
17	2 kingdoms of 6, 1 kingdom of 5	all (one person in kingdom of 5 is both YOU and TAILOR)
16	1 kingdom of 6, 2 kingdoms of 5	all (one person in kingdoms of 5 is both YOU and TAILOR)
	or 4 kingdoms of 4	all except YOU and TAILOR
15	3 kingdoms of 5	all except TAILOR

COMPLETE KINGDOM

Sentence /Sentence Fragment List

Answers are abbreviated : (K= KING; Y=YOU; S=SUBJECT; V=VERB; HV=HELPING VERB; T=TAILOR)

Jeff wanted some mayonnaise on his sandwich. (K)
In the middle of the elementary school playground. (S, V, optional HV, T)
Mary and Tom ate an extra large lunch. (K)
Running through the park. (S, HV, T)
Mr. Brown with his newspaper and magazine. (V, optional HV, T)
Stay in your seat. (K, Y)
My mother and father and the rest of the family. (V, optional HV, T)
The teachers decided about the Halloween party. (K)
Cried and cried for hours about the dog. (S, T)
On the bottom of the elephant's feet. (S, V, optional HV, T)
Jumping all the way across the lawn. (S, HV, T)
Name that tune! (K, Y)
After school last Thursday afternoon. (S, V, optional HV, T)
The dog on the sidewalk. (V, optional HV, T)
Stepping over the sleeping cat. (S, HV, T)
Lock the door now. (K, Y)
After lunch but before dinner. (S, V, optional HV, T)
Asking too many questions about the money. (S, HV, T)
Clean up your room before breakfast. (K, Y)
Amy and three of her biggest dogs. (V, optional HV, T)
Throwing balls and balloons into the air. (S, HV, T)
The antlers on the plastic deer had broken off. (K)
Eat all of your lunch. (K, Y)
Jonathan at the program last night. (V, optional HV, T)
Held a candle in her left hand. (S, T)
I like your new blue tennis shoes. (K)
At the end of each month. (S, V, optional HV, T)
Don't forget your homework tomorrow. (K, Y)
Walking through the woods on a snowy day. (S, HV, T)
Brush your teeth before bedtime. (K, Y)

*Some sentences/sentence fragments may have additional responses which must be considered if a kingdom can explain its rationale. For example, "The dog on the sidewalk" could use S, V, T. ("He allowed the dog on the sidewalk.")

MODIFICATION: Make construction paper crowns of various colors for the KINGS to wear. Kingdoms may then be named "The Blue Kingdom", "The Red Kingdom"...

READ-OUT FOR PARTS OF SPEECH

OBJECTIVES:
To improve usage and understanding of nouns.
To improve usage and understanding of pronouns.
To improve usage and understanding of verbs.
To improve usage and understanding of adverbs.
To improve usage and understanding of adjectives.
To improve usage and understanding of prepositions.
To improve usage and understanding of conjunctions.
To improve usage and understanding of interjections.
To improve analytical thinking.

TARGET POPULATION: Grades 2-5

MATERIALS: Basal reader for each student
Category list (provided)
Chalkboard and chalk

PROCEDURE: Have all students open their reading books to a designated story that they have previously read. Announce the exact pages that will be used.

Choose a category from the provided list or select any other category based on the ability and background of the class. For example, write the category "proper noun" on the board. Students then individually search their texts for words that fulfill the stated category. There will possibly be several correct responses within the selected pages. As each student finds a word that fulfills the category, she places her finger on the word and then raises her hand.

When about half of the class is ready to respond, call on one student. Ask her to state the page and paragraph where she has found her example so that other students may find it as well. Ask the student to state the word that she believes fits the category, and then to read aloud the entire sentence where the example was found. After the sentence has been read, ask if anyone has found a different example. Follow the same procedure and allow two or three students to respond to each category.

Next choose a different category and write it on the board. Use the same pages of the reading book or designate new ones. Play continues in this manner until time runs out or until everyone has had an opportunity to respond at least once.

MODIFICATIONS: This activity can be done in teams with points awarded for correctly identifying a word that fits the category. An additional point can be given if the sentence is read correctly from beginning to end.

Category List

common noun	adverb	singular pronoun	adjective
proper noun	singular noun	plural noun	conjunction
preposition	interjection	past tense verb	present tense verb
future tense verb	article	helping verb	linking verb
action verb	plural pronoun		

HANGMAN

OBJECTIVES: To review parts of speech.
To improve stategies for success.
To improve association skills.

TARGET POPULATION: Grades 2-5

MATERIALS: Sentence list (provided)
Secret Phrase list (provided)
Chalkboard and chalk

PROCEDURE: On the chalkboard draw a large picture of a set of gallows. Select a secret phrase from the provided list. On the chalkboard place a series of dashes to represent the secret phrase. Each dash will represent a blank line that will be filled with one letter. The secret phrase "ZERO DEGREES", for example, would be represented as :

_ _ _ _ _ _ _ _ _ _ _

Divide the class into two teams. Read aloud one of the sentences from the provided list. Identify one word as the target word and inform students which word that is. Reread the sentence. The first player from Team 1 must correctly identify the part of speech of the target word in the given sentence. For example, if the target word is "round" in the sentence "The round ball floated along the murky river", a correct response would be "adjective".

If the first player correctly identifies the part of speech of the target word, she earns the right to guess one letter of the secret phrase. If the letter does indeed occur in the phrase, place the letter on the proper line on the chalkboard. If there is more than one of that letter in the phrase, place all of them on the appropriate lines. For example, if the player guesses the letter "E", the secret phrase "ZERO DEGREES" will look like this:

_E_ _ _E_ _EE_

A player who guesses a letter in the secret phrase is entitled to guess the phrase itself. She may consult with teammates before making her guess. If the guess is correct, fill in all of the blanks on the chalkboard so that students can see the entire puzzle revealed.

If the player is unable to identify the correct part of speech for the target word in the given sentence, the first player from Team 2 is allowed to guess. If she is correct, she may guess a letter from the secret phrase. If she is incorrect in her attempt to identify the part of speech, play passes to the second player from Team 1, then the second player from Team 2 ... until someone correctly responds.

If a player identifies the correct part of speech, but then guesses a letter that is not in the secret phrase, she may not guess the phrase. On the chalkboard draw the next piece of the hangman figure. The parts are added in order as follows: 1) the rope, 2) a head, 3) a body, 4) an arm, 5) a second arm, 6) a leg, 7) a second leg, 8) an eye, 9) a second eye, and 10) a frowning mouth. Play then passes to the next player from the opposite team.

On the chalkboard make a list of letters which have been incorrectly guessed as part of the secret phrase. This will prevent students from guessing those same letters.

After a player correctly identifies the part of speech for the target word in a given sentence, and guesses a letter in the secret phrase, play passes to the next player from the opposite team. Choose another target word from the same sentence or a different one and continue the procedure as above.

The first round is over when the phrase is guessed or when the frowning mouth has been placed on the hangman. Award one point to the team that correctly guesses the secret phrase. Neither team earns a point if the frowning mouth is placed on the hangman.

Continue the next round by selecting a new secret phrase, drawing the dashes that represent the phrase on the chalkboard, drawing a new set of gallows, and following the procedure as described above.

MODIFICATIONS: This activity may be done without the use of the gallows. Some seasonal symbols would include: 8-10 balloons that cannot all be erased (DON'T POP THE BALLOONS); an Easter basket with erasable eggs (DON'T BREAK THE EGGS); a snowman with erasable parts (DON'T MELT THE SNOWMAN)...

This game format can be used with the sentence lists from various other lessons in this book. For example, the sentence list from NOUN, PRONOUN, NEITHER can be used to review a more limited selection of parts of speech.

Sentence List

(pron.=pronoun; adj.=adjective; adv.=adverb; prep.=preposition; conj.=conjunction; int.=interjection; h.vb=helping verb)

int. adj. adj. noun h.vb adv. h.vb verb prep. adj. noun
HOORAY, THE SILLY CLOWNS WILL SOON BE MARCHING THROUGH THE STREETS.

int. adv. prep. noun h.vb pron. verb adv. adj. noun conj. noun
WOW! WHERE ON EARTH DID YOU FIND SUCH PERFECT ORANGES AND APPLES?

int. pron. h.vb. adv. verb pron. verb pron. adv. adv. prep. adj. adv. adj. noun
OUCH! I DO NOT BELIEVE HE HIT ME SO HARD WITH THAT REALLY HUGE STICK.

pron. verb adj. adj. noun prep. adj. adj. noun conj. adj. noun verb adv. prep. adj. noun
SHE DROVE THE OLD CAR ACROSS THE DIRT ROADS ALTHOUGH THE TIRES WERE NOT IN GOOD SHAPE.

adj. adj. adj. noun prep. adj. adj. noun verb adv. conj. pron. h.vb. adv. verb pron.
THE GRUMPY OLD MAN WITH THE BATTERED SUITCASE HOLLERED LOUDLY, BUT WE DID NOT HELP HIM.

int. h.vb. pron. adv. verb adj. adj. adj. noun prep. adj. noun
HOLY MACKERAL! HAS ANYONE EVER SEEN THE HUGE SLIMEY SNAKE NEAR THE POND?

conj. adj. adj. noun h.vb. verb prep. adj. noun pron. verb pron.
ALTHOUGH FRAGRANT PINK ROSES WERE BLOOMING BESIDE THE PORCH, NO ONE NOTICED THEM.

Secret Phrase / Sentence List

Spring has sprung.
Hot chocolate
Blue skies above
Frosty the Snowman
Free as a bird
Thanksgiving feast
School's out.

Zero degrees
Sleigh bells ringing
Long underwear
Partly cloudy
School is canceled.
Harvest time
Falling leaves

Keep off the grass.
Mow the lawn.
Smell the roses.
Ring out the old.
Autumn leaves
Bread and butter
Let it snow.

PUTTING IT ALL TOGETHER

OBJECTIVES: To review parts of speech.
To increase the ability to construct grammatically correct, logical sentences.

TARGET POPULATION: Grades 3-5

MATERIALS: Parts of speech word list (provided)
Pencil and paper for each pair of students
Chalkboard and chalk

PROCEDURE: Group students into pairs or threesomes. Attempt to balance teams by ability as much as possible. Teams will be generating complete and grammatically correct sentences using provided words which will be written on the board and labeled for expected use.

On the board write the headings of the parts of speech targeted for this activity. Choose from the eight listed below. Depending on the skill level of your class, all eight parts of speech may be used, or as few as three or four. Write one appropriate word on the board under each of your targeted headings. Ask each group to construct a sentence using as many words as desired, but including all of the given words *as specified.* That is, the noun must be used as a noun, not as a verb. Nouns may be used in the singular or plural form and verb tenses may be altered. Allow time for each group to prepare a written response and then ask each group to read aloud its sentence. Write sentences on the board for critiquing.

Continue by choosing new words and following the same procedure.

MODIFICATIONS: One point can be awarded to each team for a correct sentence or for each correctly used word.

Write one word under each heading for parts of speech for a total of eight words, and challenge groups to use as many of the specified words as possible in a single sentence. Award one point for each correctly used word.

Make the activity more challenging by choosing incongruent words for the same sentence. For example, the words "rocket", "twirl", "fuzzy", and "beside" should result in some interesting sentences. Remind students that their responses must be logical.

Parts of Speech Word List

NOUNS	PRONOUNS	VERBS	ADJECTIVES	ADVERBS	PREPOSITIONS	CONJUNCTIONS	INTERJECTIONS
bear	I	smile	glittery	slowly	under	but	ow!
rocket	you	sail	hard	quickly	in	and	yikes!
sidewalk	he	fall	crowded	quietly	below	yet	zounds!
child	she	race	pointy	generously	with	or	oops!
book	it	read	romantic	silently	of	so	wow!
kitten	we	jump	soft	patiently	beyond	because	gadzooks!
flowers	they	dance	wet	never	through	since	man!
bus	me	listen	healthy	often	between	although	aah!
farmer	them	dig	deep	well	across	however	eek!
jungle	us	crash	humid	happily	during		
unicorn	him	fight	curly	always	without		

PARTS OF SPEECH REVIEW

OBJECTIVES: To review parts of speech.
To increase the ability to construct grammatically correct, logical sentences.

TARGET POPULATION: Grades 2-5

MATERIALS: Sentence formation list (provided)
Pencil and paper for each student
Chalkboard and chalk

PROCEDURE: Divide the class into three or four teams. No team member should be able to see what other team members are writing. Select one of the sentence formations from the provided list, such as "*The* adjective noun verb adverb." Write the sentence formation on the chalkboard. Tell students that in this example all sentences will begin with the article "***the***". The first person in each row will be responsible for writing an adjective for his team's sentence. The next person will write a noun. The third member will write a verb, and the fourth person, an adverb. All involved students will write their words simultaneously without the benefit of knowing what other team members are writing. When all teams are ready ask team #1 to reveal its sentence. This can be accomplished by having each person, in order, state the word he has written on his paper.

Award the team one point if all of its chosen words fit the given sentence formation. Award a second point if the sentence actually makes sense and is grammatically correct.

After hearing each team's sentence and awarding all points, continue with round two. Choose another sentence formation from the list. The team member who is next in line will write the first word of the next sentence. Continue the activity as in round one.

Play continues until time expires. The same sentence formations may be reused often, not at all, or for the entire activity. Sentences will never be duplicated because students are instructed that previously used words are not permitted to be used again, with the exception of conjunctions. The team with the most points at the end of play is declared the winner.

MODIFICATIONS:

Sentence Formation List

	Examples
Interjection *the* adjective noun verb adverb.	(Gee, the purple flower faded quickly.)
A(n) noun verb preposition *the* noun.	(A horse walked through the garden.)
Pronoun adverb verb adjective noun.	(She quickly ate green vegetables.)
Interjection helping verb pronoun verb adjective noun?	(Yuk, did he eat five worms?)
The noun conjunction *the* noun verb.	(The blender and the toaster broke.)
Adverb pronoun verb preposition *the* noun.	(Nervously we crept down the alley.)
A(n) adjective noun verb *a(n)* adjective noun.	(A lonely man watched a sad movie.)
Pronoun verb adverb conjunction adverb.	(They read slowly and carefully.)
Helping verb noun verb adverb preposition *the* noun?	(Will John run away from the dog?)
A(n) adjective noun verb preposition pronoun!	(A red bird whistled at me!)

SYMBOL SENTENCES

OBJECTIVES:
To improve usage and understanding of nouns.
To improve usage and understanding of verbs.
To improve usage and understanding of adjectives.
To improve usage and understanding of adverbs.
To improve usage and understanding of pronouns.
To improve usage and understanding of articles.
To increase the ability to construct grammatically correct, logical sentences.
To improve sentence structure.

TARGET POPULATION: Grades 3-5

MATERIALS: Symbol sentence list (provided)
Pencil and paper for each student
Chalkboard and chalk

PROCEDURE: This activity can be done with small groups working cooperatively, or by upper grade students responding individually. Place the following symbols and labels on the board and explain each one:

@ noun	/ adjective	# helping verb and/or verb
$ adverb	% pronoun	+ article (a, an, the)

Choose a symbol sentence from the provided list and write it on the chalkboard. Challenge students to create a sentence by supplying an appropriate word for each symbol. No extra words are to be added, and no words are to be left out. For example, if the symbol sentence is:

"# @ # % + / @?"

a correct response could be:

"Did Jason give him the science book?"

When each student or group is ready, ask each to read its sentence aloud. Have the class evaluate each response for fulfilling the symbol pattern and being meaningful.

When all sentences have been checked, write another symbol sentence on the board and repeat the procedure.

MODIFICATIONS: This activity could by used as a free time challenge for students.

Choose your own symbols if the ones provided do not suit you.

✋ ❖ ♈ ⌨

Symbol Sentences

+ / @ # $.
# @ # $?
/ @ # $.
@ # % + / @?
% # # $.
# $!
% # % + / @.
# % + @.
+ / / @ # $.
@ # % + / @.

APPENDIX

PARTS OF SPEECH
SAMPLE LISTS

NOUNS

freedom
prince
branch
quilt
legs
playground
clock
note
drummer
glove
fork
campground
barn
dancer
yo-yo
shirt
hammer
leash
shoebox
rack
U.S.A.
cliff
tooth
bride
donkey
library
coach
rope
knot
seed
music
beach
fog
house
teenager
flower
game
brick
store
earring
bathtub
ambulance
nurse
gift
canoe
preacher
van
cloud
TV
country
fire
branch
button
Santa
computer

VERBS

say
snap
fly
forget
sneeze
stand
catch
turn
crawl
spin
remember
pick
want
ride
hug
pull
drive
wait
leave
read
weave
climb
drive
make
swim
hear
dance
sew
eat
go
chop
write
follow
hang
wait
act
punch
race
hop
rinse
need
build
chase
scrape
march
drop
speak
get
grab
hunt
come
think
love
sit
break
listen
play
dig
change
kick

ADJECTIVES

amazing
shady
short
squirmy
smooth
classic
important
young
free
shocking
spicy
private
violent
prickly
fake
healthy
sunny
feathery
natural
exciting
shiny
scary
smelly
better
brainy
muscular
balanced
round
equal
blue
sweet
most
first
tall
golden
ancient
broken
chocolate
serious
curvy
jazzy
supreme
dark
pitted
strong
chilly
regular
brawny
huge
busy
noisy
starry
high
bald
waxy

PARTS OF SPEECH
SAMPLE LISTS

ADVERBS

always	never	eagerly	crazily	almost
purposefully	tomorrow	bravely	rudely	lightly
brightly	anxiously	dryly	playfully	often
sometimes	gently	too	confidently	slowly
privately	quite	stiffly	gracefully	sadly
later	loosely	coldly	fast	happily
very	lively	really	freely	softly
instantly	today	loudly	briskly	smoothly
suddenly	anyway	out	silently	peacefully
rudely	neatly	quickly	here	shortly

PRONOUNS

he	she	it	you	I
they	we	no one	anyone	someone
everybody	anybody	somebody	nobody	anything
us	me	him	her	them
something	everything	nothing	each	all
some	none	any	either	everyone

CONJUNCTIONS

and	but	also	although	so
therefore	except	because	or	since
because	however			

INTERJECTIONS

wow	ouch	gadzooks	mm-mm	yikes
yowch	whew	phooey	uh-oh	yippee
man	zounds	yee-haw	hooray	yes
oh	ah	eek	humph	darn
golly	heavens	cool	right	alas

PREPOSITIONS

under	in	between	above	within
inside	on	underneath	beneath	to
over	beside	near	against	among
before	after	toward	of	into
during	from	except	like	for
off	by	through	out	below
about	behind	across	at	beyond
onto	around	throughout	with	amid

NOUN TICKETS / VERB TICKETS

TICKET	TICKET	TICKET
TICKET	TICKET	TICKET
TICKET	TICKET	TICKET

PROPER PATROL
Badges

Tense Cards

past	present	future
past	present	future
past	present	future

add	discuss	chop	rub
strain	clip	reach	pass
work	set	live	reject
reduce	lose	drive	file

breathe	find	discover	collect
keep	report	dig	fold
whistle	tell	remain	bend
act	stack	fly	select

do	not	can
am	has	does
did	there	will
is	are	was
were	had	have

that	who	I
you	he	she
it	we	they
should	would	could
what	where	how

CONTRACTION ACTION

Contraction List

I'd	you'd	he'd	she'd	we'd
I'll	you'll	he'll	she'll	we'll
I've	you've	he's	she's	we've
I'm	you're	who's	where's	we're
they'd	don't	wouldn't	haven't	isn't
they're	doesn't	couldn't	hasn't	aren't
they'll	didn't	shouldn't	hadn't	wasn't
they've	can't	it's	won't	weren't
that's	there's	what's	where's	how's
who'd				

Colloquial Contraction List

what've	where've	how've	what're	who're
how're	it'd	what'd	where'd	who'd
how'd	it'll	who'll	what'll	where'll
would've	could've	should've		

BATTER UP
Subject / Verb Cards

SUBJECT =
SINGULAR NOUN
VERB =
PAST TENSE

SUBJECT =
SINGULAR NOUN
VERB =
PRESENT TENSE

SUBJECT =
SINGULAR NOUN
VERB =
FUTURE TENSE

SUBJECT =
PLURAL NOUN
VERB =
PAST TENSE

SUBJECT =
PLURAL NOUN
VERB =
PRESENT TENSE

SUBJECT =
PLURAL NOUN
VERB =
FUTURE TENSE

SUBJECT =
SINGULAR PRONOUN
VERB =
PAST TENSE

SUBJECT =
SINGULAR PRONOUN
VERB =
PRESENT TENSE

SUBJECT =
SINGULAR PRONOUN
VERB =
FUTURE TENSE

SUBJECT =
PLURAL PRONOUN
VERB =
PAST TENSE

SUBJECT =
PLURAL PRONOUN
VERB =
PRESENT TENSE

SUBJECT =
PLURAL PRONOUN
VERB =
FUTURE TENSE

HEADLINE NEWS
Newspaper Headlines

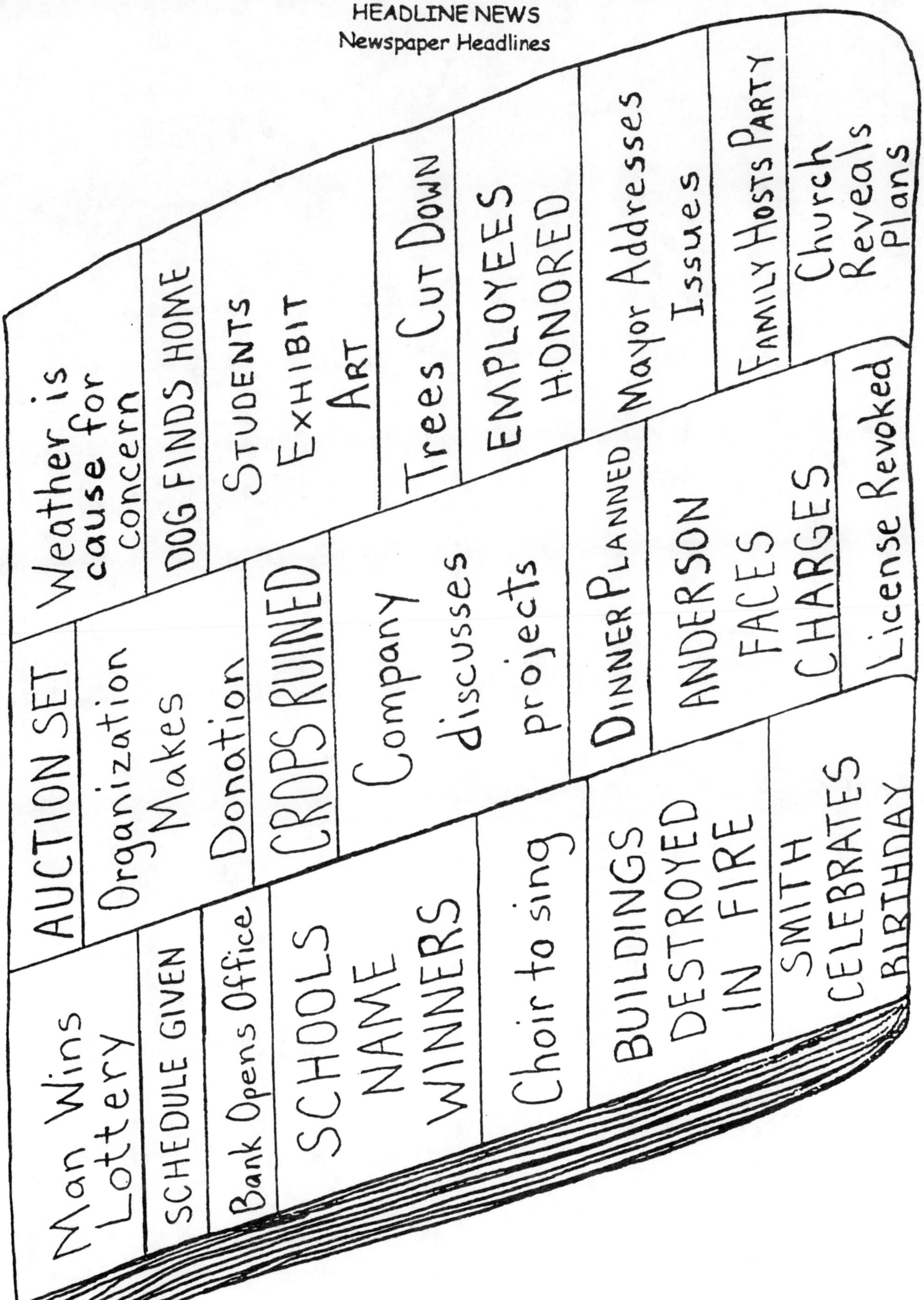

1	2
3	4

PREPOSITION POSITION
Shapes/Numbers/Letters

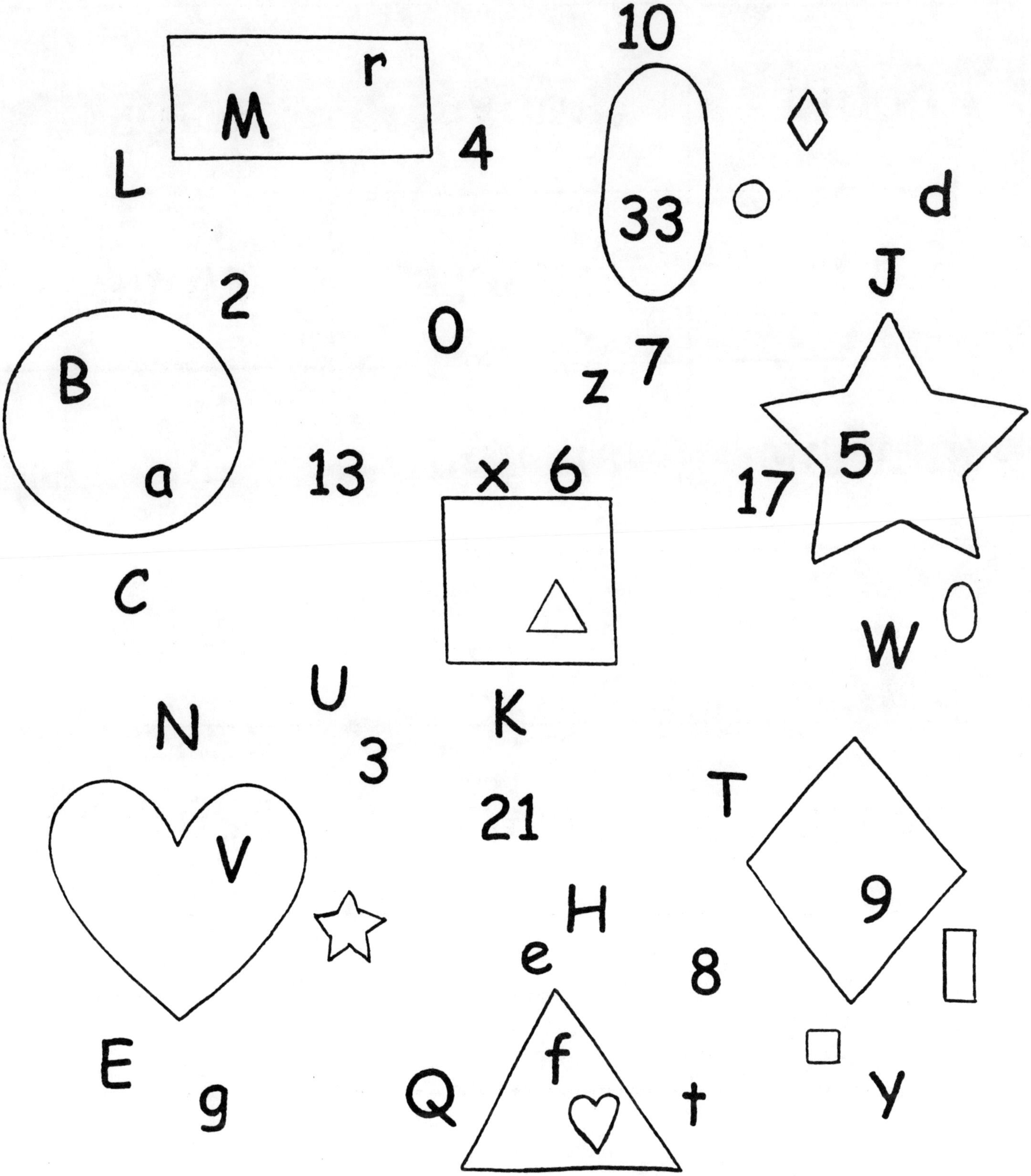

about	above	across
after	against	along
among	around	at
before	behind	below
beneath	beside	between
beyond	by	during

PREPOSITION ADDITION

Preposition Cards

for	from	in
inside	into	near
of	on	over
past	through	throughout
to	under	underneath
with	within	without

Conjunction Cards

and	or
but	however
since	although
because	so

COMPLETE KINGDOM
Job Cards

KING
SUBJECT
VERB
HELPING VERB
YOU
TAILOR